ARGUING WITH LACAN: EGO PSYCHOLOGY AND LANGUAGE

JOSEPH H. SMITH, M.D.

ARGUING
WITH
LACAN
EGO
PSYCHOLOGY
AND
LANGUAGE

YALE UNIVERSITY PRESS   NEW HAVEN AND LONDON

Published with assistance from the Mary Cady Tew Memorial
Fund.

Designed by Nancy Ovedovitz, and set in New Baskerville type by
Tseng Information Systems, Inc. Printed in the United States of
America by Book Crafters, Inc., Chelsea, Michigan.

LIBRARY OF CONGRESS CATALOGING-IN-PUBLICATION DATA
Smith, Joseph H., 1927–
Arguing with Lacan : ego psychology and language / Joseph H.
Smith.
    p. cm.
    Includes bibliographical references and index.
    ISBN 0-300-04895-5 (alk. paper)
    1. Ego (Psychology) 2. Lacan, Jacques, 1901–1981.
3. Psycholinguistics. I. Title.
BF175.5.E35S55 1991
150.19'52—dc20   90-45697
                              CIP

The paper in this book meets the guidelines for permanence and
durability of the Committee on Production Guidelines for Book
Longevity of the Council on Library Resources.

10   9   8   7   6   5   4   3   2   1

CONTENTS

INTRODUCTION

LACAN'S LANGUAGE
AND MINE

In what follows I shall address Lacan's claim that the unconscious is structured like a language, arguing that this claim is implicit not only in Freud but also in ego psychology. The argument is based on showing the difference between my own and Lacan's reading of Freud on the pleasure principle, primal repression, the unconscious in relation to language, and the ego.

Chomsky's way of phrasing the idea that the unconscious is structured like a language is that the rules (inferable only) that generate sentences (including the statements and questions in terms of which symptoms are read) are unconscious—unconscious in principle (Smith, 1978). In Freud, Lacan, and ego psychology this idea reaches to the generation of symptoms themselves. The grammar of being is unconscious. The rules of being and many of their effects operate in and appear from an other scene. Lacan calls these rules—other to me but closer to me than myself—"the Other."

Under the rule of the pleasure principle, primitive thought and action move away from danger and toward objects of desire and interest. David Rapaport was the most rigorous ego psychological interpreter of Freud. In Rapaport's understanding the pleasure principle in the broad sense is the overarching rule—the broad sense being that in which the reality principle is but a modification of the pleasure principle. That unconscious processes are structured like a language is ultimately founded on the rule-orderedness wrought by the unconscious working of psychic determinism and the pleasure principle.

To think about Lacan's assertion that the unconscious is structured like a language requires knowing how a language is structured. On that score, Lacan's point of departure was from elements in the work of Saussure, Lévi-Strauss, and Jakobson. Of course, *anything* structured is in some measure like anything else structured rather than chaotic. But what Freud taught was that primary process thinking is structured, regulated by the pleasure principle, syntactic, and thereby signifying, meaningful, semantic. So primary process thinking and imaginary modes of being (in which metonymy, wishing, symbiotic, dyadic, or dualistic modes of relating, and the drive organization of memory and anticipation prevail) are "linguistic," just as is the conceptually organized secondary process mode where triadic modes of relating prevail. The linguistic structure of the dream and other modes of primary process thinking are realized in speech and language as such in the context of secondary process thinking achieved in the oedipal overcoming of dyadic relatedness.

An individual who has achieved the symbolic mode of being has recourse to primary process thinking or thinking on the model of imaging either in the service of defense or in the service of some nondefensive project. But having recourse to imagistic or imagistically modeled thinking, whether in neurotic defensiveness or in nondefensive regression, is quite different from being limited to the imaginary—foreclosed from the symbolic. What Lacan sought to explicate was the place of symbolic castration (loss, rupture, and dividedness), of the drives, desire, and the lost object, of finitude and the name of the father, in the transition from the imaginary mode of the mirror (narcissistic) phase to the symbolic mode achieved in the oedipal era. The human is diverted from the real of bodily needs and satisfactions into the imaginary and the symbolic. He/she is subject to and subject of language.

To accept Lacan's statement that the unconscious is structured like language is one way of joining the claim that unconscious processes are rule-ordered. It is to include primary process modes of action (in the sense that imaging, thinking, and feeling are also "acts") along with secondary process modes of action within the realm of rule-orderedness. The ultimate rule of behavior, the rule inclusive of all action, all universes of discourse, is the pleasure principle, which simply states that behavior in all structural conditions moves from high to low potential. Behavior is ordered by virtue of and in the context of its being directional, dynamic. The realizations of that directionality (in more advanced levels of functioning, *intentionality*) are the lawlike effects of the pleasure principle. The reality principle is not another principle but the same principle in changed structural conditions. The infant's move from the shortest path (hallucinating the object) to the one of greater advantage (refinding the object) is the consequence of conditions having changed; anticipation has been tempered by differentiation of the "memories" of satisfaction in the form of hallucination, on the one hand, and actual satisfaction, on the other.

Lacan's statement that the unconscious is structured like a language has its validity by reason of the pleasure principle and the specifically human structural condition of linguistic competence. It embraces Freud's thought on primary process functioning and the dream work and Chomsky's (1978) on unconscious thinking and preverbal rationality. But the general statement that the unconscious is structured in accord with the lawlike effects of language, prior to delineating the specific rules of metonymy and metaphor or other structural conditions, is very close to being an alternate phrasing of the pleasure principle itself. Lacan, however, never associated his claim that the unconscious is structured like a language with the pleasure principle because, like Freud, he confused the pleasure principle with a principle of pleasure seeking; he saw it as only a regulatory principle narrowly confined (1978a:186) to primitive or regressive levels of functioning, and even, in some passages (for example, 1978a:175, 245), as a homeostatic principle of physiological functioning.

Of course, the statement of the pleasure principle and the general statement that the unconscious is structured like a language by themselves neither explain anything nor provide a sufficient basis for understanding anything. In his critique of Lacan's and Edelson's (1975) linguistic reformulations of psychoanalytic theory, Ricoeur wrote: "A decisive question for metapsychology is whether the recognition of the privileged imaginative level [that is, the imagistic or semiotic dimension] of the processes described by Freud does not make the articulation of the economic and the semiotic aspects of psychoanalysis intelligible, whereas a purely linguistic theory seems to make them almost incomprehensible" (1978:322n).

This debate can be resolved, I believe, in two steps. The first is the assumption that imagery—the semiotic, in Ricoeur's thought—though figurative (pre- or nonverbal) is significative, as Ricoeur himself insists, and thus is part of language in the broad sense. The second is the assumption of the universality of the pleasure principle, in accord with which all behavior, including every instance of imaging or speech, is directional—that is, dynamic. There can be no dynamics without economics. The specifically psychoanalytic understanding of language, then, in either the broad (that is, language taken as including imaging) or narrow sense, involves the three metapsychological points of view—the economic, dynamic, and structural.

Both Lacan and American ego psychology attempt to move away from a pseudoexplanatory overemphasis on economics. Ricoeur's effort, to my mind a perfectly valid one, is to bring the economic (and the dynamic) back into focus but in a way that avoids the hypostatization of the concepts libido and aggression, as evidenced, for example, in the notion of fusion and defusion of the drives. Regarding the latter Ricoeur wrote, "fusion and defusion are simply the correlates, in energy language, of phenomena discovered by the work of interpretation when it focuses on the area of the instinctual representatives" (1970:297). (Schafer [1968:214] similarly defines fusion and defusion in terms of compatibility or synthesis, or the lack thereof, of specific libidinal and aggressive aims.)

Lacan himself emphasized the differences between his thought and American ego psychology. In the chapters that follow I shall attempt to show the similarities. This will require highlighting the above critique of his concept of the pleasure principle and focusing on what I regard as ambiguous, fallacious, or at least disadvantageous in his concepts of primal repression and the ego. To be sure, this can be seen as an ongoing process of bending his concepts toward mine. However, one effect of that effort is an ongoing process of his language encroaching on mine. Perhaps for that reason the priority now goes to my effort to understand what *I* mean when I use Lacan's language, whether or not I use it in a way that is true to him. I can be corrected on either score (what I think or what I think Lacan thought), but attending to only my understanding of Lacan could overlook that some things in Lacan I accept and some things I don't; or that while I have learned from him, I might also, perhaps partly on the basis of that learning, have come to know some things that Lacan did not, even though I express them (partly) in his language, or, one could say, in terms that have come to be my own, stolen fair and square.

This study is also motivated by the belief that my reading of Freud, with David Rapaport and Hans Loewald as my chief guides, and my way of working with patients, while departing from Lacan's at important points, are an American reading and an American way of working that are not quite so different from Lacan's and his colleagues' as he would have had us believe. Lacanian thought need not be taken as an option over against ego psychology, as he presented it. Instead, the centrality he gave to language can be taken as a cardinal advance in ego psychology. In accord with that position, I hold that the "with" in "Arguing with Lacan" carries the sense not only of opposition but also of alliance.

When Lacan spoke of defensive ego functioning, as he often

did, he phrased it simply as "ego functioning." He did not, to
my knowledge, speak explicitly of nondefensive ego functioning. Such functioning is implied, however, in passages where
he refers to the necessity for the subject "to constitute himself in his imaginary reality" (1978a:144), to the "regulation
of the imaginary . . . [by] the symbolic connection between
human beings" (1988a:140), to the ego functioning as "a symbolic agency" (1988a:135), and to the inevitable intermingling of
the real, the imaginary, and the symbolic planes of existence.

My intention here is to coordinate what I take to be valid in
Lacan and in American ego psychology by unbracketing the ref-
erences in Lacan's work to defensive and nondefensive acts—
"acts" in the broadest sense of including any human activity. Defense (Smith, 1983) refers to actions taken to deny or disavow
danger by self-initiated distortion of inner or outer worlds. Nondefensive actions approach an object of desire or interest or, with
minimum defensive distortion, face an object of danger. Pure
forms of either defensive or nondefensive actions are theoretical
fictions.

One advantage of Lacan's concepts of real, imaginary, and
symbolic planes is that they render less likely (I *think*) reification
of the structural concepts id, ego, superego, ideal ego, and ego
ideal. "I *think*" allows for the possibility that his thought may only
bend the universal tendency to reify in different and perhaps
more interesting directions. His assumption, for instance, that the
ego ideal formed by identification with the father of individual
prehistory is the "guide governing the subject" (1988a:141) still
permits the ego ideal to be taken as homuncular agent.

The real does not refer to our imagistically or linguistically
organized and known reality. The real is that which has not been
or cannot be or resists being so organized and known. The infant's needs and also what *we* see as the objects of its environment
are real for the infant. Until its needs and objects are imagistically represented and, ultimately, symbolically articulated, the

infant is not in a world. A part of the real is referred to in Freud's statements about the infant's encounter with the mother's "unassimilable" thingliness (*Standard Edition*, 1:366).

The imaginary mode of being partakes forever of original primary narcissism. "The development of the ego consists in an estrangement from primary narcissism and gives rise to a vigorous attempt to recover that state. This departure is brought about by means of the displacement of libido on to an ego-ideal imposed from without, and satisfaction is brought about from fulfilling this ideal" (Freud, *Standard Edition*, 14:100). This text, describing a sequence in which one step is missing, is crucial to Lacan's critique of ego psychology and to his understanding of what a return to Freud would be.

The missing step is the ideal ego. The ideal ego is the idealized ego—the image of unity reflected in the mirror, the imaginary narcissistic perfection mirrored in the adoration of the mother. The ideal ego is the ego of the dyadic relationship with the early mother prior to the renunciations of the triadic oedipal crisis, renunciations that are requisite for formation of the ideal ego.

We can say that one man has set up an *ideal* in himself by which he measures his actual ego, while the other has formed no such ideal. For the ego the formation of an ideal would be the conditioning factor of repression.

This ideal is now the target of the self-love which was enjoyed in childhood by the actual ego. The subject's narcissism makes its appearance displaced on to this new ideal ego, which, like the infantile ego, finds itself possessed of every perfection that is of value. As always where the libido is concerned, man has here again shown himself incapable of giving up a satisfaction he had once enjoyed. He is not willing to forgo the narcissistic perfection of his childhood; and when, as he grows up, he is disturbed by the admonitions of others and by the awakening of his critical judgement, so that he can no longer retain that perfection, he seeks to recover it in the new form of an ego ideal. What he projects before him as his ideal is the substitute for the lost narcissism of his childhood in which he was his own ideal. (Freud, *Standard Edition*, 14:93–94)

In this sweeping passage Freud pulls together the most advanced and most primitive with at least some indications of the steps intervening. The first two sentences refer to recognizably adult, nonpathological ("one man has set up an ideal . . . by which he measures his actual ego") and pathological ("while the other has formed no such ideal") functioning. The formation of an ideal "for the ego" would refer to postoedipal repression proper, repression in response to the situations that come to be experienced as dangerous only after ego ideal and superego formation. An ideal *for* the ego (the ego ideal) replaces the prior idealization *of* the ego (the ideal ego).

The oedipal transmutation of the ideal ego into the ego ideal, of dyadic into triadic modes of relatedness, is the move from the imaginary to the symbolic realm. With this transition, a preponderance of imaginary, grandiose self-love becomes itself a danger. Once the ego ideal is formed, failure to recognize the difference between one's actual ego and one's ego ideals entails the risk of relapsing into narcissistic oneness with the mother, a merger now newly established as a danger. In addition, once the ego ideal is formed, the failure to strive toward fulfilling the ideal confronts the danger of superego attack experienced as a guilt-ridden lowering of self-esteem.

POSITIONS ORIENTING MY VIEW OF
LACAN AND EGO PSYCHOLOGY

1. A major difference—actually *the* major difference—between Lacan's language and mine is that his explicit ego concept refers exclusively to efforts to perpetuate the imaginary ideal ego. My concept of ego, the American ego psychological concept of ego, is that the changes wrought in a successfully traversed oedipal crisis result in ego-activity centrally directed

toward living up to one's ego ideal. Such an aim would always be one factor operative in and a part of the reference of the principle of multiple functioning. Since concepts are matters of definition, the question is not which is right but which is more advantageous in ordering data.

2. Some of what are perceived as differences between Lacan and American psychoanalysis are more a matter of emphasis than of substance. Lacan stressed the gap, dividedness, or lack of unity at the heart of the subject. American analysis conceives of both defensive and nondefensive ego strength or unity. The American emphasis falls on the high degree of achieved nondefensive unity required to acknowledge the immutable lack of total unity.

3. American analysts think in terms of both primitive and advanced modes of primary process thinking, either of which can be defensive or nondefensive. Secondary process thinking is advanced but it also can be either defensive or nondefensive. In the language of American psychoanalysis, Lacanian attunement to the Other (which, as Moustapha Safouan emphasizes in a personal communication, speaks in the voice of primary process) is the ongoing capacity for regression in the service of the ego (Kris, 1950). Such regression would be an instance of both advanced and nondefensive primary process thinking.

4. I am uneasy with the reifying, noun-rendering *the* in the phrase "the unconscious." While I frequently revert to that phrase here, in accord with Lacan's usage, I believe the move from the first (*Ucs., Cs.-Pcs.*) to the second topography (id, ego, and superego) warns against the *the* in favor of thinking of the unconscious quality of certain id, ego, and superego processes. To me, unconscious aspects of all three are constituents of "the" Other, with *the,* for me, again in quotes.

5. I assume that whatever is turned away from as danger or loss remains marked as an event eventually to be faced or mourned. Where the dominant motive is to repress, subordinate unconscious ego motives to track and seek out the repressed are instituted. The ego is not purely a citadel of defense.

THE PLAN OF THE BOOK

Chapter 1, "Language and Primitive Functioning," re-
lates the phylogenetic constitution of language competence to the
"prematuration" of the human infant as compared with other
animals. Prematuration in the sense of a relative absence of ori-
enting instincts also would enter into human primal repression.
I take primal repression to be the original turning away from
danger as simply too much excitation rather than any definite
"object" of danger (Smith, Pao, and Schweig, 1973). The original
turning is toward an image of the object. It is thus away from the
real and toward an image. This way of naming primal repression
places it earlier than Lacan did; in most but, as we shall see, not
all his statements on the topic, Lacan saw the turn as away from
imagery toward speech. Either definition would accord with the
notion of primal repression as the kind of repression occurring
in primary process functioning. My way of naming it would be
tied to the first instance, Lacan's to the last. The emphasis of
chapter 1 is on the preverbal organization that culminates in the
capacity for repression proper and the separateness that speech
announces. Repression proper, in which the object of danger is
more defined even if unconscious, is the kind of repression associated with secondary process functioning.

The times we play with or talk to an infant as if his or her utter-
ances were words are those intervals when the infant is not in
peremptory need and therefore is free of the binary urgency and
narrow focus on simply the object's presence or absence. Both the
peremptory and nonperemptory phases (Smith, 1976) inform
and guide development toward the preverbal higher unity of the
narcissistic or mirror stage. This is a point that will frequently
recur throughout the book.

Rather than stress the contrast between the unconscious subject of language and the conscious, defensive ego, I take the
person to be the subject of both conscious and unconscious
organization, knowledge, and desire. While Lacan differentiates

the "person" and the "subject," I maintain that both Lacan and American ego psychology study how the person/subject undertakes or avoids the task of assuming subjecthood (Lacan, 1988a:65).

In chapter 2, "The Other Scene and the Other," the pleasure principle is taken as referring to the universal movement in human intentionality from danger or disequilibrium toward an object that promises resolution or less dangerous disequilibrium. "Pleasure" in the pleasure principle refers to that goal of either primitive directionality or advanced intentionality, the achievement of which may or may not be accompanied by pleasure as an affect. The regulation or "governance" by the pleasure principle in this universal sense I take to be the presupposition of what Lacan saw as the laws or lawlike effects of language.

Lacan spoke of the lawfulness of the imaginary (1977a:141) and the necessity of imaginary competence (1978a:144). My discussion of "the order of the imaginary order" underlines that position. The imaginary is a mode of relatedness different from but modeled on what Freud called the "identity of perception," in which the image of the object is taken to *be* the object. In more advanced functioning the imaginary mode does not take the image to be the object. Separate self and object awareness are achieved. However, the imaginary persists as a dual, narcissistic, specular relatedness in which each demand (each specifically imaged or articulated wish) carries the demand for unconditional love as promise of permanent presence. The demand for unconditional love, I submit, is akin to the implicit "demand" of the identity of perception that the image *be* the object. This primitive dual mode of relatedness is overcome in the triangularity achieved by the entrance of the father and the name of the father—the father as third term in the place of the Other—in the oedipal crisis.

In chapter 3, "The Ego, Desire, and the Law," the assumption of desire is defined as the owning of want of unity. Accepting the authority of the law, assuming one's desire, accession to the symbolic order—all are accomplished in the resolution of the oedipal crisis. What is recognized in that resolution is that the incestuous impulse is a vain effort to deny the impossibility of either remerging with the mother or proceeding to some status of totalized unity apart from the mother.

Ego psychological and Lacanian concepts of ego, desire, and the law are outlined. The emphasis regarding the mirror stage achievement of a higher unity—equivalent to the higher unity of Freud's narcissistic stage and preconscious organization—is on the fact that it *is* an achievement. This is opposed to Lacan's emphasis on the potentially defensive nature, if it persists beyond its time, of the identification with the mother and the mother's mirrored picture of the infant's potential unity.

Anxiety is defined as response to danger but in the particular sense that any danger is a threat to established psychic unity. The sexual drive, Eros, strives toward ever higher unity, partly in response to anxiety over loss of unity or threat of such loss, and all the while, in response to the ultimate indestructibility of want of unity.

The law, I argue, originates in desire. Nondefensive detachment, the assumption of the authority of the law (which is to say the acceptance, ultimately, of the way things are) and the assumption of one's desire and subjecthood are achieved through recognizing the inherency of want of unity. It is the recognition of the self-annulling vanity of demand for unity (that is, the demand for unconditional love as promise of permanent presence) that brings to life both detachment/differentiation and desire. It is out of desire that the law originates; it is out of owning the indestructibility of desire that the law can be spoken. In owning a want of unity, desire achieves detachment as acknowledged want of being.

Lacan chose to assign to unconscious and conscious ego functioning the purely defensive task of maintaining an achieved false unity and attempting to ward off the undermining of that unity. My assumption that subordinate centers of disequilibrium—realized as unconscious motives to seek out all that has been turned away from—do not forever remain subordinate, together with my assumption that such seeking is a quest of the ego, is a rejection of Lacan's conceptual strategy.

Chapter 4, "Transference and Interpretation," first treats transference as a universal and then proceeds to consider certain portions of Lacan's thinking on transference. While transference was first understood to be a misreading or distortion of a new object, the current emphasis is not on transference as a *failure* in correct reading but on transference as the power to read and relate to a new object or situation in one's own way—in the light, that is, of one's prior experience. It is the power to be open to new experience in a way that not only allows the old to affect the new but also allows the new to affect the old.

Chapter 5, "The Signifying Role of Affect," discusses possible reasons for Lacan's inattention to affect and suggests a way of introducing affect into Lacanian theory differing from that of Kristeva (1983) or Green (1983). This requires a concept of the pleasure principle more clearly differentiated from pleasure seeking than that found in either Freud or Lacan. It also requires rigorous adherence—a point to which Lacan subscribed (1978a:217)—to Freud's rejection of the idea of unconscious affect. Affect has a signifying role in being the basic conscious attunement to inner and outer worlds even though it does not function as a signifier in the sense of Freud's ideation and thought or of Lacan's use of the term *signifier*. I argue that cure may be announced by an affective equivalent of facing the originally repressed signifier of one's subjecthood.

In chapter 6, "The Father of Individual Prehistory and the Ideals of the Analyst," defensive and nondefensive identifications are considered the basis for modes of allegiance among psychoanalysts to particular psychoanalytic heroes. Such allegiance is conceptualized in terms of modes that either prohibit going beyond a precursor or precisely foster such innovation. My guiding hunch is that heroes and heroines exemplify the validity of an early trust established by virtue of that which Freud named the father of individual prehistory. Freud's concept (and Lacan's concept of the paternal function) is taken as referring to all third terms that initiate and sustain early differentiation. These factors point the child toward a world beyond the dual, identificatory, narcissistic, imaginary mode of relating to the early mother. It is in this sense that the father of individual prehistory is not an object, and thus not an object for identification.

Chapter 7, "Evening the Score," is introduced by the section on "Phallocentrism, the ideal ego, and the ego ideal" in chapter 6. This final chapter, in which I resort to whimsy, plays with Kristeva's play with Lacanian phallocentrism. It is all about Eve. It is, in fact, a replaying in a lighter vein of most of the ideas set forth in the foregoing chapters.*

The individual subject matter of each chapter can be taken as variations on a theme. Lacan's thought is new enough to most readers that in approaching his concepts one must recontextualize each in terms of the others. Thus what appears as part of the frame in one context will be central in another, and what had been central will reappear in the frame of other contexts. The need for this kind of reiteration becomes even greater when one is trying to present Lacan's thought while at the same time arguing for departures from it toward ego psychological concepts of nondefensive ego functioning and nondefensive idealization, identification, and regression.

*All the chapters were written expressly for this book. However, most have been separately presented or published. Chapter 2 was presented at a meeting of *Après-Coup*, New York University, 2 December 1988. Chapter 3 was presented 22 May 1989 at a seminar sponsored by the Forum on Psychiatry and the Humanities, the Washington School of Psychiatry. Chapters 4 and 5 were presented at the Lacanian Clinical Forum at Austen Riggs Center in October 1988; a version of this material will be simultaneously published in *Psychoanalysis and Contemporary Thought* (1991, no. 1). Chapter 6 was presented at the colloquium "On Orthodoxies in Psychoanalysis: Clinical and Theoretical Implications," 14–15 January 1989, sponsored by *Après-Coup* with the cooperation of the New York University Program in Italian Studies. Chapter 7 appeared in *Modern Language Notes* (Smith, 1989).

CHAPTER ONE

LANGUAGE AND PRIMITIVE FUNCTIONING

The significance of infantile hallucinatory wish-fulfillment (inferred, of course, from dreams and other modes of regression) can be pursued in the context of a question: Are humans different from other animals because of language, or do humans have language because they are different? Normal-term humans are still in a sense subject to "premature" birth—they are born without the instincts that tend to assure survival in other species. Does this imply a phylogenetically set greater urgency of need, wish, demand, or desire? Of course, even the human infant is equipped with olfactory, tactile, auditory, and visual capacities to recognize the mother virtually immediately (Stern, 1985:47–53, 90–94). Even so, might not the "prematurity" and extreme dependency mean a less fixed, more urgent ideational or hallucinatory response to both need and the object of need?

My speculation is that the relative lack of instinctual equipment and the consequent dependency and urgency of danger and wish might, in the human infant, have intensified both hallucinatory wish-fulfillment *and* the necessity of differentiating hallucination from perception—and both of these from imaged memory and anticipation. These differentiations are accomplished within primary process thinking, and with their achievement a first-level differentiation of self and object is established. Since this is still at a preverbal level, the identity of thought thus established could be called, in contrast to the prior identity of perception, a perceptually effective identity. The identity of thought, that is, is perceptually effective as the capacity to recognize the perception of the present object as percept and the image of the absent object as image.

Speculation and inference about primitive steps leading toward language could be thought of as counter to ideas considering language as innate—that is, as not congruent with the fact that the human infant born in a language-speaking community will speak late in the first year of life. However, as Piaget (1971b:90) wrote, "even when a trait is recognized as hereditary, the question of its formation remains." Piaget emphasized equilibration processes that yield necessities in accordance with "the general laws of organization by which the self-regulation of behavior is governed" (p. 90); he further held that "the acquisition of language presupposes the prior formation of sensory-motor intelligence, which goes to justify Chomsky's ideas concerning the necessity of a prelinguistic substrate akin to rationality" (p. 91).

Chomsky (1978), like Freud, has no hesitancy in inferring unconscious thinking. "It" thinks. For Lacan, "It" speaks, or, more to the point, through "It" the Other speaks. One could also say that, because of unconscious openness to the "impressions of life" (*Standard Edition*, 14:190), "It" is written. "It" is not an empty slate but is nevertheless a locus in which traces of those impressions are inscribed. However, by virtue of the active unconscious scanning of self and world, one would also have to say that "It" reads.

In accord with the linguistic implications of these assumptions, Lacan's central inference is that the unconscious is structured like a language; at one point he even goes so far as to assert that "the unconscious *is* language" (1977a:288). He has wavered a bit between, on the one hand, claiming that this is a return to Freud's pre-Saussurian, prestructuralist understanding of the linguistic organization of the unconscious and, on the other, presenting this assertion as an instance of what Harold Bloom (1973) would call a strong misreading of Freud: "The unconscious is not Freud's; it is Lacan's" (Lacan, *Ornicar?*, as cited in Vergote, 1983:193).

The validity and fruitfulness of the claim that the unconscious is structured like a language hinge on the issue of whether something like a language can precede speech—whether the universals of the structure of language (universal grammar) also constitute the structure of primary process ideation, the conscious mentation that we assume to be the nearest reflection of unconscious thinking.

Does language exist prior to words? Is there such a thing as preverbal linguistics, notwithstanding the seemingly oxymoronic surface structure of that phrase? In adopting such an assumption would we be returning via Lacan to Freud or detouring away from Freud and toward Lacan? And does Lacan's transmutation of "the other scene" into "the Other" mean that he sees the unconscious not only as structured like a language but also as more open than conscious thought to the symbolic order of the linguistically constituted world? Heidegger (1962) wrote of Being-in-the-world as referring both to the worldhood of the world as the totality of established significance (pp. 145, 192, 231, 344, 417, 474) and to the "for-sake-of-which" of "Being in" (pp. 185–87). Is it by reason of its greater attunement to these dimensions that Lacan sees the unconscious as capable of emitting messages that do "not come from a subject beyond language, but from speech beyond the subject" (1977a:214)? Finally, in what way was Freud's unconscious (or Lacan's, to the extent that it differs) a discovery and in what way an inference?

I suggest that these speculations (maybe Freudian, maybe Lacanian, and, either way, maybe with a Smithian twist) are worthy of play. But before we can play with them or let them play with us, we have to get beyond the ordinary way of thinking of language simply as words.

One way we know that primary process thinking in images (and thus unconscious thinking, as the beyond of primary process, conscious thought) is *not* like a language in any ordinary sense is that it is not constrained to the defiles of a system of words of a community of speakers where each word, by convention and arbitrarily, is assigned an agreed-upon meaning. But might not that lack of constraint, the freely mobile displacements and idio-syncratic condensations, be a means of more intricate and immediate attunement to the world and to particular interpersonal situations in the world than can be achieved by secondary process thought? Could not this be the basis for Rorty's (1986:7) claim that "a witty unconscious is necessarily a linguistic unconscious" (the unconscious is a linguistic "partner who feeds us our best lines") and for Eliot's (1950:10) that "The bad poet is usually unconscious where he ought to be conscious, and conscious where he ought to be unconscious"?

Here is Lacan's phrasing: "At the level of the unconscious there is something at all points homologous with what occurs at the level of the subject—this thing speaks and functions in a way quite as elaborate as at the level of the conscious, which thus loses what seemed to be its privilege" (1978a:24).

Doesn't the claim that the unconscious is structured like a language naturally accord with the idea of unconscious thoughts made manifest by the dream work? The infant's disequilibrium as represented by imagery and affect, already putting into play the primarily autonomous capacities for perception, memory, ideation, affect, and anticipation, together with the absence of the mother constitute a system structuring primary process thinking. No one knows the form taken by what we think of as the contents of the unconscious. But if we are going to talk about unconscious thinking at all, it seems only a modest inference to assume that it is, like conscious primary process thinking, structured.

A diachronically and synchronically structured system that generates meaning and emits messages is like a language, and maybe it even *is* language. And the particular system under discussion, this "it," speaks, not just, as in Lacan's emphasis, in those messages that are the royal road to the dynamically repressed, such as dreams, slips, jokes, and symptoms, but all the time. In a major way it is structuring this sentence.

Let me pose the claim that the unconscious is structured like a language against the pair of claims that language is unconscious and that consciousness is structured by language. About language and words, Chomsky wrote:

> If we know only that language consists of words, our performance models would necessarily be very primitive and of restricted interest; we could study the sequence of linguistic signs and their formal and semantic properties, but nothing else. With a richer theory of competence that incorporates structures of greater depth and intricacy, we can proceed to more interesting performance models.
>
> . . . .
>
> If work of recent years is anywhere near the mark, then a language is generated by a system of rules and principles that enter into complex mental computations to determine the form and meaning of sentences. These rules and principles are in large measure unconscious and be-yond the reach of potential consciousness. Our perfect knowledge of the language we speak gives us no privileged access to these principles; we cannot hope to determine them by introspection or reflection, "from within," as it were. (1978:11–12, 17–18)

Where Lacan writes of the unconscious as structured like a language he is referring centrally to the repressed (for example, *Séminaire* I [1975:100], as cited in Felman, 1987:124). My emphasis here is on the kind of thing that Piaget (1973) termed the "cognitive unconscious" and Chomsky "unconscious knowledge," and on Freud's point that the repressed and the unconscious do not coincide: "Everything that is repressed must remain unconscious; but let us state at the very outset that the repressed does not cover everything that is unconscious. The unconscious has a wider compass: the repressed is a part of the unconscious" (*Standard Edition*, 14:166).

Freud made no attempt to characterize the basic nature of the psychical. He did deny the equation between what is psychical and what is conscious: "No; being conscious cannot be the essence of what is psychical. It is only a *quality* of what is psychical, and an inconstant quality at that—one that is far oftener absent than present. The psychical, whatever its nature may be, is in itself unconscious and probably similar in kind to all the other natural processes of which we have obtained knowledge" (*Standard Edition*, 23:283).

Freud also wrote:

The data of conscious self-perception . . . have proved in every respect inadequate to fathom the profusion and complexity of the processes of the mind, to reveal their interconnections and so to recognize the determinants of their disturbances. . . . Reality will always remain "unknowable". The yield brought to light by scientific work from our primary sense perceptions will consist in an insight into connections and dependent relations which are present in the external world, which can somehow be reliably reproduced or reflected in the internal world of our thought and a knowledge of which enables us to "understand" something in the external world, to foresee it and possibly to alter it. . . . In psycho-analysis . . . we have discovered technical methods of filling up the gaps in . . . consciousness. . . . In this manner we infer a number of processes which are in themselves "unknowable" and interpolate them in those that are conscious to us. And if, for instance, we say: "At this point an unconscious memory intervened", what that means is: "At this point something occurred of which we are totally unable to form a conception, but which, if it had entered our consciousness, could only have been described in such and such a way." (*Standard Edition*, 23:196–97)

To further show that Freud is still the father of Lacan and Chomsky, his concept of endopsychic perception can be cited. Endopsychic perception refers not to direct conscious perception but to the indirect effects of unconscious knowledge. It is "the obscure recognition . . . a recognition which, of course, has nothing in the character of a [true] recognition . . . of psychical factors and relations in the unconscious" (*Standard Edition*, 6:258). It is the "conscious ignorance and unconscious knowledge" (p. 258) of motivations, of repression (*Standard Edition*, 9:51), of what is repressed (*Standard Edition*, 10:164), and even of the "structural conditions" of mind (*Standard Edition*, 13:91).

PREVERBAL ORGANIZATION

Primary process functioning is not simply random ideational and affective experience awaiting organization into secondary process functioning. A great deal of organization occurs in the context of primary process functioning. This preverbal, primary process organizing paves the way for language and secondary process functioning, but it also founds the capacity both to return to primary process activity and to recognize, understand, and appreciate the products of primary process discovery and invention in others.

Freud conceptualized preverbal organization in terms of the autoerotic and narcissistic phases, the preconscious organization (which can be taken as synonymous with preverbal organization) and the differentiation of the ego from the id. He spoke of the narcissistic phase as a higher unity (*Standard Edition*, 14:77). Lacan's mirror stage, approximately corresponding to the narcissistic phase, is also described as the assumption of a unity, albeit the false one that Lacan saw as the beginning of the ego as citadel of defense. "Preconscious organization" (along with such other concepts as an organization with a constant cathexis, a dominant mass of ideas, defense, censorship, ego instincts, secondary process, and the reality principle) can be taken as a precursor concept of Freud's fully developed concept of the ego. I mention these concepts in order to point toward Freud's assumption of progressive organization occurring prior to the appearance of speech and in order to examine the role of repression in the achievement of that organization.

I suggest that primal repression as the very first turning away from danger (danger undefined in the mind of the infant and in the form simply of too much excitation; *Standard Edition*, 20:94) be taken as the whole class of repressive phenomena prior to the achievement of the still preverbal narcissistic, preconscious, or ego unity. The degree of organization implied by such unity allows for repression proper. In repression proper, that which is dangerous has achieved clearer definition as that which threatens the achieved unity. Both that which is turned toward and that which is turned away from are more defined and structured as compared with more primitive mentation.

Although I will later point out exceptions, Lacan for the most part locates primal repression as occurring with the onset of speech. This, as I have suggested, is another way of naming a whole class of repressive phenomena, but in terms of the end rather than the beginning of the dominance of primal repression. For him it is the advent of speech that marks primal repression and the differentiation of need, demand, and desire.

Demand I take to be the wish that can be definitively imaged or articulated. Desire I take to be the indestructible remainder of want that exceeds the fulfillment or gratification of any particular wish. Desire arises from unsurpassable wanting—wanting that pertains to coming into being as a separate individual and to the concern about that separate being. Desire, to vary the title of Judith Viorst's important statement on mourning (1986), arises from necessary lostness. As the manifestation of a want of being beyond any specific wish/demand—a want of being tied to original and ongoing loss as such rather than to any specific loss— desire is there from the beginning even though definitive differentiation of desire and demand awaits speech and, ultimately, the oedipal resolution.

Desire comes to be known by reason of representation (image or word) that substitutes for and in that sense spells the death of the thing. The image and the imager, the word and the speaker, are thus diverted, alienated from the real. Representation (language in the broad sense, understood as structuring both primitive imaging *and* speech) brings desire to light. Representation is a sign from the start that every turning away is in some sense loss, dividedness, and castration. The achievement of separateness in which all such early turnings eventuate is itself a loss of symbiotic oneness, the culminating symbolic castration preliminary to speech. Although it may be awakened and, in that sense, "caused" by a particular object, desire—finally caused by unsurpassable want of being, by the lost object in the sense of Lacan's *objet a*— is always there, hidden in the wishes that Lacan characterizes as demand: "[The effects of the signifier] proceed from a deviation of man's needs from the fact that he speaks, in the sense that in so far as his needs are subjected to demand, they return to him alienated. . . . That which is thus alienated in needs constitutes an *Urverdrängung* (primal repression), an inability, it is supposed, to be articulated in demand, but it re-appears in man as desire (*das Begehren*)" (1977a:286).

In primal repression the need-representing psychic disequilibrium is the thing as danger that is turned away from in the drive toward the object—the drive as represented in the demand that we ordinarily call the wish in the form of image or word. Both the need and its first level of representation, the drive (Lacan's concept of desire overlaps but does not coincide with his concept of drive), are "alienated" in being represented by the second level of representation, the representative image or word as wish/ demand (along with affect, which Lacan here, characteristically, does not mention).

The concept of desire highlights the emphasis in Rapaport and Loewald on the drive as being on the mind side of the mind/ body border. In an animal destined to speak, the drive does not simply represent the physical need. It is the first step into the alienation from need and thus into the dividedness, the want of being and the desire to be suffered in a linguistically constituted world. Although Lacan speaks of a possible "inability" of desire "to be articulated in demand," the image of wish-fulfillment—the demand—is, first of all, a negation, a denial of need, drive, want of being, desire, the absence of the object. Desire first "appears" as negated in wish-fulfillment.

Lacan wrote of desire as the beyond of demand (1977a:286). It is, he said, "neither the appetite for satisfaction [need], nor the demand for love, but the difference that results from the subtraction of the first from the second" (p. 287).

It seems to me reasonable that the capacity to own or disown wanting differentiated into demand and desire could not precede the advent of speech. However, the differentiation of perception of the object, on the one hand, and wish as imaged, on the other, is already there in the achievement of the identity of thought, a process of differentiation that leads to the still preverbal narcissistic or mirror stage as the preconscious organization.

Preconscious organization precedes and allows for language. The idea that preconscious organization is constituted by language as such (language in the narrow sense, language as realized in verbal speech) is anchored in all those passages in which Freud, according to Rapaport (1957–59:159), "went hog-wild" in giving verbal traces a paramount role in preconsciousness; see, for example, Standard Edition, 1:364–65, 14:201–04, 19:20. However, reliance on those passages would have to ignore the late statement in An Outline of Psycho-Analysis (1940) where that position was modified. Freud there took preconscious organization as that which was accomplished preverbally. As I read him, it is this preverbal accomplishment that allows for speech. The presence of speech is, then, a sure sign that preconscious organization has been established. "It would not be correct, however, to think that connection with mnemic residues of speech is a necessary precondition of the preconscious state. On the contrary, that state is independent of a connection with them, though the presence of that connection makes it safe to infer the preconscious nature of the process" (Standard Edition, 23:162).

It should be noted that even Freud's early statements about word-representations were almost invariably associated with the idea of hypercathexis in the sense of a higher level of organization (for example, Standard Edition, 14:194). The gist of his thinking was that knowledge, beyond the simplest level, was knowledge of relationships (*Standard Edition*, 5:530–31, 14:202; see also Gill, 1963:28–29), and that it is through language that at least a certain class of higher-level relationships is revealed.

Both primary repression and repression proper are a turning away from danger. These turnings both organize the psyche and reflect its organization, a progressive organization that allows for greater definition of danger, the self-object, the object, and the self.

Primal repression is characteristic of primary process functioning. To instantiate how this system works, Freud pictured what he took to be its most primitive form, which I interpret as follows:

1. Mounting physiological disequilibrium evokes psychic disequilibrium.
2. Psychic disequilibrium (a first level of representation, a certain quota of which will, in the mother-infant interaction, come to be organized as the drives) evokes a turning from that disequilibrium as danger toward an image of the object (a second level of representation—the image [and the affect accompanying it] that represents the drive).
3. The image, presumably of such urgency in the human infant as to take hallucinatory form, is the identity of perception, a wish-fulfillment.
4. The turning away from danger as undefined disequilibrium, or "too much excitation," structures an ongoing tendency to anticipate and avoid such danger. However, in the human, an opposing though subordinate tendency is also established to seek out and integrate or face or mourn that which has been turned away from as dangerous or as lost.
5. The hallucination gives momentary, wish-fulfilling gratification. It is worth pausing here. Gratification, even though initially momentary, is in the image of the other, even though not yet known as other. One could even think that it is here that desire as desire of the Other begins. The connection of image

as (pre)signifier with a concept of the object as (pre)signified constitutes the first (pre)sign. Gratification in the sign, precursor of the word, together with both the dominant tendency to seek out the object turned toward and the subordinate tendency to face that which has been turned away from, are the factors that combine to divert the human toward and into language.

6. The more urgent the danger the more brief is the moment of wish-fulfilling gratification. Since the hallucinatory image does not actually satisfy, it becomes associated with the danger, becomes a danger itself, and is accordingly turned away from. Hallucination, then, is marked as danger, and there is a turning toward the indicators of reality marking the actual object (the identity of thought) and the actual satisfaction it affords.*

If the goal here were tracing the first steps toward adapting to a fixed biological reality, one could end with that Freudian sketch. The goal instead is to understand how the human infant, repeating ontogenetically what was phylogenetically set, gets diverted from the real into imagery and language, through which, eventually, a linguistically constituted reality or world is established.

The turn away from hallucination toward the actual object marks the point at which hallucination and image are differentiated. An image of the object can be recognized as not bearing the indicators of reality of the object as present. And even when disequilibrium is mounting and satisfaction is delayed, the image is not marked as a danger, as was the hallucination, but as the signpost leading toward a refinding of the urgently needed actual object.

*The fact that hallucination recurs in psychic states is an indication of how dangerous "reality," in terms of the psychic interpretation of the subject, has become.

PEREMPTORY AND NONPEREMPTORY NEED

Up to this point I have focused on the situation of peremptory need and danger. This is to be contrasted with the situation of nonperemptory need and minimal disequilibrium, such as after awakening but before need has mounted to a peremptory level, after feeding but before falling asleep, and during sleep. While the infant is awake at such times there is no hallucination, if waking hallucination can reasonably be taken as response to urgency of disequilibrium and danger. There is instead imaging, perhaps kaleidoscopic imaging, but imaging that affords more than just momentary gratification because of the unpressured situation. Here the infant can play with images. Freud wrote: "If we do not require our mental apparatus at the moment for supplying one of our indispensable satisfactions, we allow it itself to work in the direction of pleasure from its own activity. I suspect that this is in general the condition that governs all aesthetic ideation" (*Standard Edition*, 8:95–96).

Play with images, though at an earlier level, is similar to what Langer emphasized as the human tendency to babble, to play with sounds, as a precursor of speech. The image of the object represents the infant's disequilibrium. But at the nonperemptory point of play, the disequilibrium is neither urgent nor narrowed to only one need. An image of the object here would unite self and object and, simultaneously, allow for the differentiation of self and object. A whole world of imagery is opened up in which both self and other belong and are represented, but nevertheless it is a world *between* self and other. It is a world that signifies escape from the binary urgency and narrow focus on simply the object's presence or absence.

It is a world accessible to the infant not only in a nonperemptory waking moment but also during sleep. Assuming that peremptory disequilibrium would cause awakening, the hallucinatory vividness of the imagery in dreams is not an indication of urgent danger but simply a regression to the state of organization in which hallucination and image were not differentiated.

To speak of a regression to an earlier state of organization points toward the progressive organization that occurs in the context of primary process thinking prior to speech, an organization that culminates in the self and object differentiation that the advent of speech announces. The free play of imaging in the nonperemptory moment is still just as much under the regulation, as we say, of the pleasure principle as imaging at the peremptory moment. It is just that there are less urgent and more varied loci of disequilibrium that motivate a turning away from and turning toward. In both cases the pleasure principle system is the same.

But how can we conceive of the way in which progressive organization and integration are fostered by primary process thinking in both the peremptory and nonperemptory moment? It is the same as the example of Freud's identity of perception and identity of thought interpreted above. However, it can be pictured in more advanced form. This requires conceptualization in terms of unconscious impulses, wishes, images, thinking, memory, and anticipation, even though, as has been mentioned, there is no way of knowing what shape or form such inferred contents or processes of the unconscious might have. All we can say, with Freud, is that in order to put our inferences into words, we can only translate "back into the language of our perceptions, from which it is simply impossible for us to free ourselves" (*Standard Edition*, 23:196).

Freud also maintained, so far as the dynamic unconscious is concerned, that "only something which has once been a *Cs.* perception can become conscious" (*Standard Edition*, 19:20, 237). I take him to mean that whatever has been repressed was at one time represented by an image. That is to say, whatever form and organization the contents of the dynamic unconscious might have, Freud assumed the organization of such contents to be modeled on the primitive conscious mode of thinking in images. That primitive modes of thinking are unconsciously maintained is no bar to the possibility of unconscious contributions to the solution of complex problems.

PREVERBAL KNOWLEDGE AND THOUGHT

Let us picture, then, primitive unconscious thinking and repression as they might be thought to occur in the narcissistic or mirror stage, meaning at a point prior to speech but after the preconscious as an organization (which I will take here as the higher unity equivalent to the ego) has been structured. As Freud pictured it in "Repression" (*Standard Edition*, 14:149), an impulse—an impulse that would spell danger—achieves or begins to achieve representation as an image that Freud named a wish. This evokes, it is commonly assumed, an anxiety signal from the ego, and the image representing the impulse is repressed. The disequilibrium that gave rise to the impulse continues (as does the subordinate ego impulse to seek out that which has been turned away from) and, because of delay, is intensified so that it achieves or begins to achieve representation by another image. Since the dominant impulse is to ward off danger, the second image will be one that presents the impulse in a modified, less dangerous mode. But perhaps that, too, and subsequent images that are even more modified will still be marked as dangerous and be repressed. Finally, an image that represents the impulse in a way that does not evoke repression will be admitted to consciousness.

The chain of "images" thus unconsciously established will persist as a source to be called upon when the danger that forbade their entry to consciousness is no longer a danger; these images will break through in symptoms or in dreams, slips of the tongue or pen, or in humor, even when the danger persists as a danger; and they will appear in moments of regression in the service of seeking out all that has been turned away from. This is my understanding of what Lacan meant by unconscious signifiers and, in part, how it is that unconscious knowledge exceeds conscious knowledge.

But the last assertion deserves some qualification. As Piaget (and Sartre, to whom he refers) observed, that which is dynamically repressed is unconscious only by virtue of the "subject's connivance" (Piaget, 1971a:135).* That which we have repressed we sort of know, whether we can directly think about it or not. Clinical practice relies heavily on that assumption. It also explains how insight often arrives as affectively charged recognition of something one has "known all along."

This would imply that although the data inscribed by reason of unconscious openness to the bodily mediated impressions of life would far exceed that portion that can enter the defiles of consciousness, the organization of consciousness is paralleled by organization of the unconscious. Unconscious knowledge exceeds that of consciousness, but without consciousness, without the preconscious organization that parallels unconscious organization, the store of unconscious knowledge would be utterly useless and meaningless. Without a conscious "I" to own or disown its own unconscious knowledge and desire, speaking of an unconscious "I" is senseless. Whether defensive or not, consciousness—or, as Freud put it, "the property of being conscious or not"—remains "our one beacon-light in the darkness of depth-psychology" (*Standard Edition*, 19:18).

Owning or disowning one's unconscious knowledge and desire is both a conscious and an unconscious process. Resolution of the oedipal crisis that allows for the assumption of symbolic castration, finitude, separateness, gender, and desire—what Lacan called the assumption of the law of the symbolic order—involves at each step of the way both conscious and unconscious owning. That is why the first topography had to give way to the second. "I" am the subject of everything to which the concepts id, ego, ego ideal, and superego refer. And if those concepts prove to be

---

*I would put it this way: that which is dynamically repressed is so because of unconscious ego activity that both tracks the repressed and prohibits conscious awareness of it.

inadequate, as they surely will, they can be discarded in favor of others. That is what Lacan is about in his concept of the subject, of the Other as the locus of the signifier, and the unconscious as structured like a language. "The Other is the locus in which is situated the chain of the signifier that governs whatever may be made present of the subject—it is the field of that living being in which the subject has to appear . . . it [is] on the side of this living being, called to subjectivity, that the drive is essentially manifested" (1978a:203).

CHAPTER TWO

THE OTHER SCENE
AND THE OTHER

THE PLEASURE PRINCIPLE AND
THE LAWS OF LANGUAGE

"The other scene" was Freud's term for the scene of
unconscious processes, the scene of the drives, of the dynamically
repressed, and of primitively organized primary process functioning. The name first given to the other scene was "the *Ucs.*,"
later changed to "the id," and even later, by at least Lacan, to "the
Other." But Freud, even at the beginning, never took the *Ucs.* to
be simply a seething cauldron.

The primitive, preverbal organization, Freud believed, is
based on a phylogenetically set response to psychic disequilibrium as danger that institutes a quest for the mother, even though
the mother is not yet known as other. The principle of such regulation was thus called the unpleasure principle—later the pleasure principle.* Psychic disequilibrium can arise from bodily dis-

---

*In the pleasure principle as a principle of homeostasis, "unpleasure"
is the name assigned to psychic disequilibrium and "pleasure" the name
assigned to the relative lack thereof. Neither should be taken as affects.
It is true that the names derive from the fact that the consciously noted
effects of disequilibrium are often affectively signaled by unpleasure,
and manifestations of that unpleasure are the mother's surest guide to
the infant's distress. However, as a regulatory principle, the pleasure
principle refers also to psychic disequilibrium that is neither consciously
registered nor associated with unpleasure as an affect.

equilibrium or from bodily mediated events in the environment.
Consciousness at this preverbal level is restricted to percepts,
global feelings of pleasure or unpleasure, and thinking/wishing/
fearing in images rather than words. An image of the object
(meaning a fragmentary memory of a prior perceptual/affective
experience of the mother) arises in the mother's absence and at
first falsely (hallucinatorily) signifies her presence. As we have
seen, Freud called this confusion of image and object, taking the
image to *be* the object, the identity of perception.

In terms of primitive organization, the fact that this is a false
connection is less important than that it *is* a connection of image
with object. It is not yet a sign because the image is not fixed
(in the next instant another image can refer to the same object),
arbitrary, or conventional but fluid and idiosyncratic. However, it
foreshadows language. In Saussurian terms, the image as the signifier is thus joined, just as one side of a sheet of paper is "joined"
to the other, with a primitive concept of the object as the signified
even before the infant can know that the evanescent (pre)sign
thus formed refers to the mother as other. The infant is on its way
toward language. Primitive imagery consisting of freely mobile
displacements is already joined to a primitive concept (memory
and anticipation) of the object.

Without the mother's absence, without delay in the gratification of need, the false connection constituting the identity of
perception would not occur. The mother's absence together with
the false connection is the essential start toward the eventual
capacity to imagine and to think in words—the adult capacity for
linguistically based, logically constrained, temporally organized
secondary process thought.

Hallucinatory wish-fulfillment is already an experience of the
object in its absence. Condensations and displacements are never
really random; directional (dynamic), they carry meanings that,
though consciously unknown to the infant, reflect the organization of and further organize the presubject and his or her world.
A positive consequence of hallucinatory wish-fulfillment is that
the human has the opportunity and is compelled to sort out the

difference between wish-fulfillment and actual satisfaction, between an idea of the object and the actual object.

In the ordinary reading of Freud on these matters it is understood that one gets one's bearings by overcoming the primary process mode of thinking in order to find, to refind, the object as such. But if primary process thinking can be taken as a manifestation of language in the broad sense, if imagery *is* a language in the narrow sense, then, like any language it is complete; it says it all, even at the initial point where the "lexicon" is limited to one image. The image is still the manifestation of a signifying system (cf. Lacan, 1988b:29, 30, 33, 76). As indicated above, the system structuring primary process thinking is constituted by the infant's disequilibrium as represented by imagery and affect (already putting into play the primarily autonomous capacities for perception, memory, ideation, affect, and anticipation) together with the absence of the object. If this be so, one's initial bearings are established not by overcoming such thinking but within and by virtue of that thinking and the systematization it reflects. Language as such and secondary process thinking come later and signify that organization to the point of self and object differentiation has already occurred.

I wrote above of Piaget's emphasis on equilibration processes that yield necessities in accordance with "the general laws of organization by which the self-regulation of behaviour is governed" (1971b:90). Analysts will be reminded of all those solid-sounding, comforting passages wherein Freud assures us of the invincible governance of the pleasure principle. (The reality principle, which Lacan, according to Muller and Richardson [1982:63], hands over to the ego as a defense, is, after all, merely the operation of the pleasure principle in changed structural conditions, and *Beyond the Pleasure Principle* is not beyond the principle but merely beyond pleasure seeking [Smith, 1977].) To speak of governance might suggest that the pleasure principle is an agency that governs, an idea comparable to thinking of the law of gravity as an agency that makes apples fall. But laws of nature are simply clear statements about how things work, how elements of a system interact, perhaps how they interact to go in a certain direction. The pleasure principle is just such a statement.

For Lacan, that which structures the human and the human world consists of the laws of language. The other scene is the locus of language, which he termed "the Other." Lacan's way of phrasing that the law of the Other, beyond its representatives (mother, father, analyst, God), is only to be discovered and is neither made nor imposed by an agent is as follows:

> Let us set out from the conception of the Other as the locus of the signifier. Any statement of authority has no guarantee [other] than its very enunciation, and it is pointless for it to seek it in another signifier, which could not appear outside this locus in any way. Which is what I mean when I say that no metalanguage can be spoken, or, more aphoristically, that there is no Other of the Other. And when the Legislator (he who claims to lay down the Law) presents himself to fill the gap, he does so as an imposter.
>
> But there is nothing false about the Law itself, or about him who assumes its authority.
>
> The fact that the Father may be regarded as the original representative of this authority of the Law requires us to specify by what privileged mode of presence he is sustained beyond the subject who is actually led to occupy the place of the Other, namely, the Mother. The question, therefore, is pushed still further back. (1977a:310–11)

> The Other . . . the locus in which is constituted the I who speaks to him who hears . . . extends as far into the subject as the laws of speech, that is to say, well beyond the discourse that takes its orders from the ego, as we have known ever since Freud discovered its unconscious field and the laws that structure it. (1977a:141)

I wish "its unconscious field" referred to the ego, the conscious, defensive ego, but, of course, in Lacan it refers always to "the Other." The ego, in Lacan, is essentially a structure of defense. The ego and its imaginary objects, the ego and its dual relationships (meaning defensively identificatory, closed off from the Other, without access to the symbolic father in the locus of the Other), stand between, transverse, and impede the discourse between the analyst in the place of the Other and the unconscious subject of the analysand, also in the place of the Other. The analyst, Lacan wrote, "should be thoroughly imbued with the radical difference between the Other to which his speech is addressed, and that second other who is the individual that he sees before him, and from whom and by means of whom the first speaks to him" (1977a:140).

So, there is the "I" as ego and the "I" of the unconscious subject of language. But let us follow Lacan to see not only the possible price paid but also the advantages gained from that conceptual splitting.

Is what thinks in my place, then, another I? . . .

In fact there is no confusion on this point: what Freud's researches led us to is not a few more or less curious cases of split personality. . . .

The end that Freud's discovery proposes for man was defined by him at the apex of his thought in these moving terms: *Wo es war, soll Ich werden.* I must come to the place where that was.

This is one of reintegration and harmony, I could even say of reconciliation (*Versohnung*).

But if we ignore the self's radical ex-centricity to itself with which man is confronted, in other words, the truth discovered by Freud, we shall falsify both the order and methods of psychoanalytic mediation. . . .

The radical heteronomy that Freud's discovery shows gaping within man can never again be covered over without whatever is used to hide it being profoundly dishonest.

Who, then, is this other to whom I am more attached than to myself, since, at the heart of my assent to my own identity it is still he who agitates me?

His presence can be understood only at a second degree of otherness, which already places him in the position of mediating between me and . . . my counterpart.

If I have said that the unconscious is the discourse of the Other (with the capital O), it is in order to indicate the beyond in which the recognition of desire is bound up with the desire for recognition. In other words this other is the Other that even my lie invokes as a guarantor of the truth in which it subsists.

By which we can also see that it is with the appearance of language the dimension of truth emerges. (1977a:171–72)

So much for Lacan's rebuttal of the idea of "another I." Clearly, he is not talking about split personality; he is instead conceptualizing a central issue of human heteronomy. However, he is still involved, not just metaphorically but conceptually, in thinking of an "I" of the ego over against another "I," the unconscious subject of language (cf. Gallop, 1985:155–56).

Before proceeding to his treatment of the ego and the imaginary order, let us listen to one of Lacan's summary statements of what he meant by "the unconscious is structured like a language":

> The laws of recollection and symbolic recognition are, in effect, different in essence and manifestation from the laws of imaginary reminiscence. . . .
> To touch on the nature of symbolic memory, it is enough to have studied once . . . the simplest symbolic sequence, that of a linear series of signs connoting the alternative of presence and absence. . . . One then elaborates this sequence in the simplest way, that is, by noting in it the ternary sequences in a new series, and one will see the appearance of the syntactical laws that impose on each term of this series certain exclusions of possibility until the compensations demanded by its antecedents have been lifted.
> With his discovery of the unconscious . . . Freud was taken at once to the heart of this determination of the symbolic law. For, in establishing, in *The Interpretation of Dreams*, the Oedipus Complex as the central motivation of the unconscious, he recognized this unconscious as the agency of the laws on which marriage alliance and kinship are based. (1977a:141–42)

Well, that rather says it all. It is the structuralist view. The statement might seem to blur, as many passages in Freud do also (Smith, 1978), the distinction between unconscious in principle and unconscious in fact, between the cognitive unconscious (Piaget, 1973) and the repressed. But one could argue that the laws of language, while unconscious in principle, nevertheless structure the repressed, and for Lacan they structure not only the repressed but also consciousness, the oedipus complex, and the cultural order.

THE ORDER OF THE IMAGINARY ORDER

In the passage cited above Lacan begins by stating that "The laws of recollection and symbolic recognition are . . . different . . . from the laws of imaginary reminiscence." One might expect Lacan to nail down that contrast by discussing the essence and manifestation of lawfulness in each realm. Instead, beyond mentioning "the echo of feeling or instinctual imprint" (p. 141) that characterizes the imaginary, he leaves aside lawfulness in the imaginary, writes only of the lawfulness of the symbolic, and from there proceeds directly to the oedipus complex as the central motivation of the unconscious and the unconscious as the agency of the laws of marriage alliance and kinship.

It should be noted that he does attribute lawfulness to both the symbolic and the imaginary—as opposed to the real, which he elsewhere (1977b:11) characterizes as not an order, implying the absence of law. My understanding is that the symbolic and imaginary are two different "languages," each having its own rules of grammar but both sharing the universal lawfulness of the pleasure principle. The advent of speech is the consequence of new organization, new structural conditions in which the rules of pleasure principle regulation change in the direction of what Freud conceptualized as the reality principle. The question left unanswered in the passage cited, it seems to me, is this: How is it that imaginary capability, imaginary competence, the structuring of the imaginary order, is a necessary preliminary to speech and thus to any possibility of oedipal accession to the symbolic order?

Here I must backtrack. I wrote above of language in the broad sense, language that includes imaging as, in the nonperemptory moment, a form of play, and I speculated that humans are phylogenetically and ontogenetically diverted into language by reason of their comparative prematurity. If so, who could count it as other than a lucky diversion away from the real (of bodily need and satisfaction) into the imaginary? But I also wrote that, notwithstanding the freely mobile displacements and the wider response to more varied centers of disequilibrium, such non-peremptory primary process thinking is still organized by the law of the pleasure principle. The gist of my argument is that Lacan specified this lawfulness, explicitly in the realm of the symbolic and implicitly in the realm of the imaginary, as the laws of language. Displacement and condensation (metonymy and metaphor) occur in accord with the pleasure principle as a universal.

Prior to his Rome Report in 1953, Lacan "regarded the 'imago' as the proper study of psychology and identification as the fundamental psychical process. The imaginary was then the world, the register, the dimension of images, conscious or unconscious, perceived or imagined" (Sheridan in Lacan, 1977a:ix). With the ascendancy of the symbolic in Lacan's thought from 1953 onward, the imaginary was reduced to a function of the ego as citadel of defense, with virtually all modes of identification taken as instances of such defense. The ego itself was then taken as that imaginary, false sense of unity (which forever tends to preserve itself) achieved by identifying with the bodily unity reflected by the mother or the mirror during the mirror stage, when the child is eight to eighteen months.

Lacan's ego, *le moi*—the "me" that every child utters before saying "I" (but neither "me" nor "I" before saying "mama")—together with its images and dual relationships, constitutes the imaginary relation. But even when the child says "I" it is still the ego, that imaginary unity achieved and defended, which speaks. Lacan's "I," *le je,* is the unconscious subject of language, the unconscious subject in the locus of the Other.

Every psychoanalyst has some way of phrasing, if only to himself or herself, the daily practice of listening to the "I" behind the "I" that is speaking—a practice that applies both to listening to the analysand and to listening as an analyst to oneself. But

Lacan's notion of the unconscious subject of language is radical. The signifier, adapted from the sense developed by Saussure and Jakobson, represents the subject for another signifier. The signifier, for Lacan, floats free of not only the usual tie to a referent but also Saussure's sense of the signified. Signifiers acquire value only in their relations with each other. The system of signifiers—language—is the symbolic order. Here it would not be quite right to speak of the signifier that represents a subject to another signifier as "my" signifier; "I" as the unconscious subject of language am an effect of the signifier, beneath which "I" fade.

I have argued above that language in the broad sense must be taken as structuring primitive imaging just as effectively as it structures speech. It is by virtue of both the imaginary and the symbolic that the real can come to be encountered as real. Imaging and speech, in that event, would be two separable linguistic categories. The lawfulness of each category would be more clear in terms of a concept of the pleasure principle as a universal rather than, as in Lacan, a homeostatic principle guided by pleasure and unpleasure as affects. The consequence of that conceptual lack is that Lacan's dominant exposition of the imaginary and of ego functioning (what I call defensive ego functioning) is in terms of a persistence beyond its time of a denial of symbolic castration (permanent loss and dividedness), together with the defensive identifications (dual relationships) that tend to bolster such denial. This emphasis is crucially important. It does, however, tend to leave out the role of nondefensive primary process functioning. But by virtue of the system structuring primary process thought, the first image is an image of a remembered (and anticipated) experience of satisfaction. Those passages in which Lacan speaks of an "irreducible, non-sensical" signifier and "the logical necessity of that moment in which the subject as X can be constituted only from the Urverdrängung, from the necessary fall of this first signifier" (1978a:251), I read as follows: A first signifier, a first image, would appear without the infant having either conscious or unconscious knowledge of its signified or referent.

However, by virtue of the system of need, absent object, and innate capacities, we can say that the signifier does, nevertheless, carry meaning beyond that which is accessible to the infant.

A first signifier that intimates the subjecthood of the subject, prior to any other signifiers that carry the same intimation with which the first could come into relation, is repressed. It is repressed because it is nonsensical (nothingness) and yet intimates separateness and loss of symbiotic unity. That repression is the inaugural act of the subject as subject. The subject comes into being through negation, through repression of the very signifier that announces its subjecthood. The founding act is a kind of suicide.

Encountering the signifier that first announces one's subjecthood is to experience one's thrownness, empty-handed, into the world. The idea that the empty signifier that announces nothingness nevertheless carries the meaning of subjecthood and world is a bit like saying that in one's thrownness one is, nevertheless, in the hand of God. As I shall discuss in chapter 6, the idea of a sustaining structure of meaning beyond one's conscious or unconscious grasp can be taken, I believe, as the most basic level of meaning in Freud's concept of identification with the father of individual prehistory.

THE EGO AND THE OTHER

Of course, the concepts of the imaginary and the symbolic convey some kind of tie with primitive and (if beyond its time) defensive functioning in the case of the imaginary and nondefensive functioning in the case of the symbolic. That is understatement. No matter the categories initially chosen or altered, they would inevitably be enriched by a clinician as brilliant as Lacan over a lifetime of work with patients. It remains up to those who follow after him to decide whether his initial conceptual choices match the insights accomplished in his work.

My own judgment is that while his "I" as the defensive ego,

differentiated from the unconscious "I" of the subject, matches
in an important way the metaphorical thinking of every clinician,
it can be faulted as a less parsimonious theory than the concept
of functions that can be deployed either consciously or unconsciously and either defensively or nondefensively—functions to
which the concept of ego is usually assigned. It is a concept that
allows for the idea of intrastructural conflict.

This was Freud's concept of the ego, and it did not and does
not cover over man's radical heteronomy nor the task of "where
id was it is my duty to come into being." If Lacan thought his
own concepts more aptly covered all that of which "I" am the
subject, and particularly pictured the unconscious more aptly
than Freud's concepts of id, ego, and superego, then he should
have dispensed with them and substituted his own. Instead, he
wrongly insisted that Freud's concept of ego was Lacan's own
conception of the ego as citadel of defense.

So much for what I regard as the price paid for his splitting
of the "I" into two, the defensive "I" of the largely conscious, defensive ego and the unconscious "I" of the subject. What might
be considered the advantages?

Unconscious knowledge of oneself and one's world always exceeds that which can be gleaned and synthesized from the defiles
of consciousness. But with Lacan's concept of the Other the idea
of "my" unconscious knowledge gets turned around. It is not so
much that "I," even unconsciously, have knowledge of the Other;
the Other structures me. That is, by virtue of the mediation of
the Other, we are led "to attain . . . not that which can be the object of knowledge, but that . . . which creates our being and about
which [Freud] teaches us that we bear witness to it as much and
more in our whims, our aberrations, our phobias and fetishes, as
in our more or less civilized personalities" (1977a:174).

The Other, Wilden maintains, cannot be defined "in any definite way, since for Lacan it has a functional value, representing
both the 'significant other' [for example, mother in the place of
the Other] to whom . . . demands are addressed (the appeal to the
Other), as well as the internalization of this Other (we desire what

the Other desires) and the unconscious subject itself . . . (the unconscious is the discourse of—or from—the Other)" (Wilden in Lacan, 1968:263–64). The unconscious is transindividual, intersubjective, not just in being "that part of the concrete discourse . . . which is not at the disposition of the subject to reestablish the continuity of his conscious discourse" (p. 265)—a statement prior to Lacan's devising the concept of the Other. It is transindividual in that the system that structures me includes the mother in the place of the Other and later the father and the name of the father as the metaphor of the paternal function.

The preconscious organization achieved prior to speech is a first-level differentiation from the mother, but the relationship with the mother remains not only an intense object tie but also an identificatory mode of relatedness (that is, the dual mode that Lacan calls "imaginary") until the oedipal resolution. It is during the oedipal assumption of symbolic castration, gender, finitude, one's desire as indestructible, and one's subjecthood as marked by lack that non-identificatory intersubjectivity is established. The oedipal transition allows for an ongoing acknowledgment that one is not the author of one's being, which is the foundation for an ongoing nonidentificatory, intersubjective way of life in the light of the Other.

Felman wrote:

What matters, in Lacan's perception of the Oedipus as constitutive of the qualitative difference between the Imaginary and the Symbolic, is the fact that the triangularity of the Symbolic narratively functions as the story of the subversion of the duality of the Imaginary. The Oedipus drama mythically epitomizes the subversion of the mirroring illusion through the introduction of a difference in the position of a Third: Father, Law, Language, the reality of death, all of which Lacan designates as the Other constitutive of the unconscious (otherness to oneself) in that it is both subversive of and radically ex-centric to the narcissistic, specular relation of self to other and of self to self. (1987:105)*

*For a brief explication of the father, the name of the Father, and the Law, see Felman, 1987:168n, and on the unconscious as the discourse of the Other, pp. 120–28.

CHAPTER THREE

THE EGO, DESIRE,
AND THE LAW

> An essential component of [the] experience of satisfaction is a particular perception . . . the mnemic image of which remains associated thenceforward with the memory trace of the excitation produced by the need. As a result of the link that has thus been established, next time this need arises a psychical impulse will at once emerge which will seek to re-cathect the mnemic image of the perception and to re-evoke the perception itself, that is to say, to re-establish the situation of the original satisfaction. An impulse of this kind is what we call a wish. (Freud, *Standard Edition*, 5:565–66)

WISHING AND DESIRING

Primitive thinking in images is wishing. The image of the object and the affect accompanying it represent a need for the object. Thought, indistinguishable in this primitive form from wishing, is evoked by need. If the need is urgent, peremptory, so also will be the wish. With the acquisition of speech, thinking is usually (though not always) at the language-based, relatively neutral, logically constrained, and temporally oriented secondary process level. Secondary process thinking is not unmotivated, but the element of wishing usually derives from interconnected "higher level" areas of disequilibrium of such minimal urgency, at such a remove from basic needs and drives, that it appears neutral. In that sense, it resembles the relatively neutral imaging of primitive nonperemptory experience.

Relatively neutral adult thought even in the face of urgent need is a capacity assured by achieved ego autonomy. In the infant, the relatively neutral imaging of the nonperemptory experience is entirely dependent on the absence of urgent need.

"Wish" corresponds closely to Freud's *Wunsch*. However, French translators, as Sheridan tells us, "have always used '*désir*', rather than '*voeu*', which corresponds to '*Wunsch*' and 'wish', but which is less widely used in current French. The crucial distinction between '*Wunsch*' and 'wish', on the one hand, and '*désir*', on the other, is that the German and English words are limited to individual, isolated acts of wishing, while the French has the much stronger implication of a continuous force. It is this implication that Lacan has elaborated and placed at the center of his psycho-analytic theory. . . . Furthermore, Lacan has linked the concept of 'desire' with 'need' (*besoin*) and 'demand' (*demande*) in . . . [a particular] way" (in Lacan, 1978a:278; cf. Lacan, 1977a:256–57).

Desire thus encroaches, to its advantage, I believe, upon the language of Freud. It takes over or specifies the idea of continuous force in Freud's idea of the indestructibility of unconscious wishes (Lacan, 1978a:31) and infringes in various ways upon the concept of libido, as it also does on Freud's Eros. Needs—bodily needs, physiological disequilibrium—are represented first as psychic disequilibrium, which in turn is primitively represented at the level of ideation and affect. Demand refers to the articulation of a specific wish. The meaning of "articulation" here not only refers to the verbal utterance of a demand but also includes the image as an article of signification. Preverbal steps in differentiation and integration would depend on progressive establishment of relationships between such articles of signification.

I can adopt Lacan's terminology and call the flow of images a flow of signifiers if his terminology can be adapted to my insistence that no "signifier" can exist independently of a signified, even if, in primitive imaging, the signified is not yet known. In that sense they are like, or are primitive forms of, what Saussure called the "signs" of language as such. The fact that in primary process thinking there is no convention assigning such signifiers to a fixed referent still leaves room for Lacan's idea of a flow of the signified beneath the signifiers, that is, the same signified may at the next moment be tied to a different signifier. But at the moment of its appearance, no signifier can be devoid of connection with that which it consciously or unconsciously signifies. Perhaps the criterion is met in Lacan by the fact that the signifier represents the subject. In any event, the criterion also leaves room for Lacan's insistent stance that signification is constituted, the signified and its referent brought to light, only by virtue of the relationships established between signifiers.

The meaning, the signified and referent, of a signifier would be consciously unknown, and in that sense not yet established or constituted, in the mind of the infant. Such meaning can only come to light by virtue of the signifier being or becoming a link in a signifying chain. We can go further: on the assumption that even unconscious knowledge is subject to progressive organization, the newborn infant would not even unconsciously know the meaning of a signifier. But the meaning is there, constituted by the system of need and absent object of need, awaiting the light of unconscious or conscious recognition. Imaging, if not yet intentional, is at least directional. It is regulated by the law of the pleasure principle.

Lacan wrote of "Desire . . . crossing the threshold imposed by the pleasure principle" (1978a:31). This statement, the paragraph in which it occurs, and similar passages elsewhere repeatedly show that Lacan took the pleasure principle to be a homeostatic principle guided by pleasure and unpleasure as affects. Rapaport (1960:875–77) wrote that the pleasure principle is "the most frequently and most radically misunderstood psychoanalytic concept" (p. 875; see also 1953:504; Rapaport and Gill, 1959:802). In accord with his statement that the pleasure principle "has not *per se* anything to do with pleasure or pain" (1957–59, 1:74), Rapaport argued that "the constancy principle, the nirvana principle, and repetition compulsion are manifestations of the pleasure principle under various structural conditions" (1960:877). I have argued (1977) that the clearest manifestation of the pleasure principle under changed structural conditions is the reality principle. Rapaport was clear as to how the pleasure principle must be understood through a reading of Freud with an eye for that which can be maintained as internally consistent. Hartmann (1956:249)* and Lacan were not.

*In "Dualism Revisited: Schafer, Hartmann, and Freud," I wrote of what Hartmann *should* have said about the pleasure principle: "It could have gone something like this: 'Actually there aren't three regulatory principles and, to tell the truth, there aren't even two. All that talk about the pleasure principle being modified into the reality principle was just a shorthand way of referring to changed structural conditions. But we now have other more varied and more precise concepts that refer to these changed conditions, e.g., change of function and secondary autonomy, concepts that can be applied to particular aspects of development.' He might have continued: 'The point is that the system does have self-regulative capacity, i.e., a drive goes toward discharge unless delayed and when thought or action crosses a perimeter of danger it will be delayed. The nature of and motives for delay vary vastly between primitive and advanced functioning, and we should avoid naming a new regulatory principle for each developmental step. That leaves us with the pleasure principle which is, unfortunately, badly named because it invites attribution of agency, aim, and bias to the regulatory principle itself. However, Freud had a way of saying "and then the pleasure principle took over" with such a compelling ring (like Yahweh saying "let there be light") that it is hard for all of us not to follow along. Perhaps it would be preferable to speak neither of regulatory principles nor even of a regulatory principle, and instead specify how self-regulative capacity continues through changed danger situations and structural conditions, but beginning right at birth, on the drive/defense or drive/control model of the anxiety signal. In fact, this is what I have done'" (Smith, 1986a:559).

Although I return repeatedly to it, I must now depart from this discussion of the pleasure principle and pursue what I regard as the important Lacanian distinction between demand and desire.

Lacan argued that demand, while being a specific, articulable wish, is also always implicitly a demand for unconditional love and that satisfactions of such specific wishes are taken as tokens of such love (1977a:265, 286, 311)—tokens, I would say, of an impossible love, love as promise of permanent presence.

No doubt we can in some way attribute such a wish to the all or none desperateness of the infant in a state of urgent need, but to think of the infant taking satisfaction as anything more than just satisfaction of the specific need and wish implies a unity achieved beyond the most primitive level. I would suggest that specific demand begins also to carry the demand for unconditional love at the point at which a higher level of unity, a first level of infant/ mother differentiation, is established as the preconscious organization, in the still preverbal, mirror (narcissistic) stage.

Of course, it would still be adultomorphic attribution to believe that the preverbal infant could harbor so synthetic an idea as unconditional love. However, by virtue of language, and language in the broad sense, the human comes into being as a creature concerned about its being. Each primitive step toward unity and separateness is a step in the heightening of that concern no matter its mode of representation in the mind of the infant. The first level of that unity and that concern manifests itself only as an undefined wanting, but a wanting beyond merely the satisfaction of bodily needs. By inference from later stages of development, such "surplus" wanting can be read as the initial indicator of the demand for unconditional love. That dimension of demand is by virtue of language; it could only come to pass in a creature destined to speak. It is a level of demand that both covers and heralds the coming to light of the desire that marks the subject as subject of language.

As mentioned above, my emphasis here regarding the mirror

stage achievement of a higher unity is that it *is* an achievement, as opposed to Lacan's emphasis on the potentially defensive nature, if it persists beyond its time, of the identification with the mother and the mother's mirrored picture of the infant's potential unity. / One way of explicating the Lacanian maxim that desire is desire of the Other is that while the establishment of preconscious organization is a step toward differentiation of the self and other, as a first level of unity it is more a recognition of the mother-infant unit than of one's self as a unity. And, even in recognition of the mother-infant unit, the accent, as in Kohut's (1971) concept of the self-object,* would be more on the object, the mother, than on the self. Since thinking begins in the form of images of the object, it would naturally follow that the object comes into focus prior to any primitive mode of self-reflective awareness (Freud, *Standard Edition*, 4:61; and 5:574, 615–16; Piaget, 1971a:47, 135; Chomsky, 1968:26, 43, 103, 173).

Lacan's gloss on the idea behind these Freud, Piaget, and Chomsky citations regarding the object's coming into focus prior to any primitive mode of self-reflective awareness is in terms of a barring or fading or eclipse or splitting of the subject. Kristeva wrote:

> Lacan discovered in *fantasy* the exemplary efficacy of the object 'a' [*objet a*] since in his view the structure of fantasy is linked "to the condition of an object . . . the moment of a 'fading' or eclipse of the subject that is closely bound up with the *Spaltung* or splitting that it suffers from its subordination to the signifier" [Lacan, 1977a:313]. That is what is symbolized by the formula, ($ ◊ a) where ◊ indicates desire. (1987b:387)

---

*Kohut's self-objects are the primitive objects (e.g., the "idealized parent image," 1971:26) not yet constituted as separate. Of course, as Loewald (1973:449) observed, the self-object nature of such early objects would also characterize the not-yet-differentiated self. Kohut acknowledged (1971:xx) that the self-object concept, along with those of mirroring and the mirror transference, significantly overlaps Lacan's thought. (See Kerrigan's comment, 1983:xiii.)

The question, though, is the ultimate place of the object after separateness (object and self awareness) has been established. Lacan's central mode of addressing the fate of the object was by means of what he called the *objet a*. The *objet a* is that dimension of any object which evokes desire beyond any specific demand and also beyond the demand for unconditional love. With the advent of desire, the persistence of prior demands for unconditional love is revealed as a fetishistic effort to fill an unfillable lack—to deny separateness and also to deny any inner gap or dividedness. Love as desire acknowledges that the immutable separateness of the self and the object is matched by immutable inner lack in the self and the object.

LACK AND ANXIETY

Of course, wanting beyond the demand for satisfaction of immediate and pressing need—"surplus" wanting—is already manifested in the less urgent wishes followed out in relatively neutral nonperemptory imaging. It would be in these phases, relatively free of urgent and narrow focus on the object of need *as* object of need, that various attributes of the mother could come into focus and be integrated in some primitive concept of the mother as a unity. But such a development would foreshadow or intimate in some primitive way the separateness also of the self. If anxiety can be taken as the response to threat to an achieved psychic unity, such an intimation of separateness would evoke the inaugural experience of anxiety. Conceiving of the mother as a unity, a part of which would be recognizing, as Freud put it, the mother's "unassimilable" thingliness (*Standard Edition*, 1:366), would be a threat to the symbiotic unity. At that point each wish, each demand, addressed to the mother would carry also the demand for unconditional love as a promise of permanent presence.

Regarding the infant's jubilant identification with its mirror image, Muller and Richardson (1982) wrote that the identification camouflages (p. 6) or, alternatively, overcomes (p. 66) the anxiety of bodily fragmentation. Both terms, I believe, hold. The identification is jubilant because it is the achievement of a level of unity. The anxiety, partly overcome and partly camouflaged, is, I would say, anxiety in response to a prior symbiotic unity lost. It is lost by reason of the inexorable differentiations that are the effects of the laws of language. It is the higher unity intimated in glimpsing the mother's separateness (implying one's own) that, first of all, disrupts the prior unity and evokes anxiety. Anxiety about bodily fragmentation already implies a preconscious organization, an ego as the seat of anxiety (*Standard Edition*, 20:93, 104, 140, 161). The jubilance is partly a response to unity reestablished (anxiety overcome) and partly manic-like denial of the anxiety that accompanied the transition and anxiety persisting because, to the extent that the higher unity is based on the false identification, it is already under siege (anxiety camouflaged). But, fundamentally, any higher unity is besieged because it is forever less than total unity.

Let us assess the possible advantages of exploring the definition of anxiety as response to danger but in the particular sense that any danger can be a threat to established psychic unity. The portion of primitive wanting that becomes, in interactions with the mother, organized into libidinal drive would be wanting that pertained to the preservation or reestablishment of psychic unity. Freud took to be sexual all primitive wanting not directly tied to the satisfaction of physical needs. He also spoke of something "in the nature of the sexual instinct itself" (*Standard Edition*, 11:188) that fosters sublimation, a going beyond itself "along other paths" (*Standard Edition*, 21:105). The sexual drive, Eros, strives toward ever higher unity, partly in response to anxiety signaled by the loss of a prior unity and partly in response to the ultimate indestructibility of want of unity. Even the desire for sexual union itself is the playing out of the desire for reunion with the other, for unity with the other. It is in the light of these factors that I understand Lacan's statement, "One can see how the sexual relation occupies this closed field of desire, in which it will play out its fate" (1977a:287). Lacan wrote: "Desire begins to take shape in the margin in which demand becomes separated from need: this margin being that which is opened up by demand, the appeal of which can be unconditional only in regard to the Other, under the form of the possible defect, which need may introduce into it, of having no universal satisfaction (what is called 'anxiety')" (1977a:311).

The concluding brief aside on anxiety in this passage identifies anxiety as response to the loss or threat of loss of unity and selfsameness introduced by delay—the inevitable delay in the satisfaction of need.* Such an interpretation accords with Lacan's comments on the lack of anxiety in Melanie Klein's apathetic four-year-old patient: "It is clear in fact that in Dick what is not symbolized is reality. This young subject is entirely in crude reality, reality unconstituted. He is entirely in the undifferentiated. . . . Anxiety is what is not produced in this subject" (*Séminaire I*, 1975:81–82, as cited in Felman, 1987:112).

This passage and Felman's comments accord with the idea of anxiety as response to the loss or the threat of loss of psychic unity, whether or not the absence of manifest anxiety in Dick is seen as defect or defense. Lacan and Felman see it as developmental defect. I see it as a mixture of defect and defense, which is to say I see "entirely in crude reality" and "entirely in the undifferentiated" as Lacan making his point, as he often did, with hyperbole. But whether defense, defect, or both, Dick is effectively "defended" against any danger that would threaten his quite primitive level of unity and stability. No anxiety, no anxiety signal, is evoked. Laplanche and Pontalis (1973:103) define defense as a "group of operations *aimed at* the reduction and elimi-

---

*Delay, of course, along with the innate capacities, is the third term that introduces everything: anxiety, imaging, affect. Delay introduces the turn that is not just toward the object but also, in her absence, toward the whole chain of signifiers that represent and substitute for the object.

nation of any change liable to threaten the integrity and stability of the bio-psychological individual." Anxiety would be the
response to any danger that threatened Dick's primitive unity.
Felman wrote:

> How should we account now for the salutary emergence of Dick's
> anxiety? Anxiety is linked to the Symbolic: it is the way in which the
> introjection of the symbolic system *as a whole* makes itself felt in the sub-
> ject, when any element in it is disturbed or displaced. Anxiety occurs
> with the assumption of difference (castration), not simply because of the
> imaginary fear that something (death, or loss of bodily integrity) might
> happen to the subject, but because of the symbolic recognition that, since
> everything is not the same and since every disturbance is reverberating
> in the whole symbolic constellation, the situational givens that affect the
> subject do make a difference (meaning). (1987:116–17)

If we take the libidinal and aggressive drives as equiprimor-
dial (and on the mind side of the body-mind border), their force
in primitive mentation must be assumed as joined, operative in
an identical direction. If primitive aggression can be defined as
efforts to distance or destroy an object of danger (Smith, Pao,
and Schweig, 1973), then the aspect of flight away from a source
of disequilibrium would be the anlage of the aggressive drive and
the aspect of flight toward the object the anlage of the libidinal
drive. Flight away from a source of psychic disequilibrium evoked
by need can be conceived as flight from a threat to or a loss of
unity. Anxiety does not invariably occur, but when it does it is the
conscious signal or concomitant of that threat.

I have repeatedly emphasized that the human comes into being
as a psychic unity not just by virtue of a false mirroring, but by
virtue of language in the broad sense, through which a higher-
level, more complex unity is actually established. In addition, I
stated that, by virtue of language, the human comes into being
(comes into being as a psychic unity, even though that unity is
marked by lack and dividedness from the start and forever) with
concern for that being.

Lacan wrongly understood American psychoanalysis as promoting ego autonomy in a way that covers over immutable lack at the heart of the self. I have stressed that the opposite is true. The difference between Lacan and ego psychology is not that between an emphasis on lack in Lacan and an emphasis on unity in ego psychology; the essential difference is that ego psychology acknowledges both defensive and nondefensive unity and holds that the deepest concern for one's being and for one's want of being is dependent on the achievement of nondefensive unity. Only on the basis of such unity can one acknowledge the inevitability of lack, loss, and limit.

DESIRE AS THE OWNING OF WANT OF UNITY

Desire can be taken as a manifestation of the concern about one's being. Let us then define desire as the wanting that pertains to the continuation of unity established or to the reestablishment of unity—typically a higher, more complex unity—after a prior unity is lost. Since any human unity is always marked by dividedness, always under siege, always lacking, concern and desire are constant. But at the point of recognizing desire as manifesting an indestructible want of unity, anxiety in response to specific dangers is rendered less blind and less driven, by virtue of being coordinated with the detachment achieved in acknowledging concern as constant.

Lacan, forever fond of putting things in enigmatic nutshells, held that "the desire that is to be recognized" is "the desire of recognition" (1977a:141). "Desire is the metonymy of the want-to-be" (1977a:259, 274).

Desire is produced in the beyond of demand, in that, in articulating the life of the subject according to its conditions, demand cuts off the need from that life. But desire is also hollowed within the demand, in that, as an unconditional demand of presence and absence, demand evokes the want-to-be under the three figures of the nothing that constitutes the basis of the demand for love, of the hate that even denies the other's being, and of the unspeakable element in that which is ignored in its request. In this embodied aporia, of which one might say that it borrows, as it were, its heavy soul from the hardy shoots of the wounded drive, and its subtle body from the death actualized in the signifying sequence, desire is affirmed as the absolute condition. (1977a:265)

Lacan also wrote of "the desire that presents itself as autonomous in relation to this mediation of the Law, for the simple reason that it originates in desire, by virtue of the fact that by a strange symmetry it reverses the unconditional nature of the demand for love, in which the subject remains in subjection to the Other, and raises it to the power of absolute condition (in which 'absolute' also implies 'detachment')" (p. 311). I read this as a statement that the law originates in desire; the oedipal assumption of the law is also at once the assumption of one's desire and subjecthood. Nondefensive detachment is achieved through recognizing the inherency of want of unity. The fundamental law is not the law against incest. The law against incest can be broken. The fundamental law is not legislated or laid down, not contingent. It is subject neither to change nor infraction but is immutably the way things are. What is recognized in the resolution of the oedipal crisis, as I commented earlier, is that the incestuous impulse is a vain effort to deny the impossibility of either remerging with the mother or proceeding to some status of totalized unity apart from the mother. This recognition of the self-annulling vanity of demand brings to life both detachment and desire. It is out of desire that the law originates; it is out of owning the indestructibility of desire that the law can be spoken. It is through desire that one learns that the law is love.

With a machine, whatever doesn't come on time simply falls by the wayside and makes no claim on anything. This is not true for man, the scansion is alive, and whatever doesn't come on time remains in suspense. That is what is involved in repression.

No doubt something which isn't expressed doesn't exist. But the repressed is always there, insisting, and demanding to be. The fundamental relation of man to this symbolic order is very precisely what founds the symbolic order itself—the relation of non-being to being.

What insists on being satisfied can only be satisfied in recognition. The end of the symbolic process is that non-being come to be, because it has spoken. (Lacan, 1988b:307–08)

Anxious, automatic flight from danger, Freud taught, yields to a facing of danger and a judgment about it. The detachment achieved by owning the inherency of want of unity is precisely the presupposition of such judgment. It is this nondefensive detachment that renders one more tolerant of anxiety, less disposed to either hysterical or obsessional modes of pretending that one is in possession of such unity, less phobic or persecuted, and less disposed to depressive claims that the lack of unity and love as permanent presence is due to one's badness—a merely contingent fault in one's self.

Subjecthood refers to the potentiality of the person to own existing in the face of death, marked by insurmountable lack of unity, centeredness, or completeness. In this owning, wish or demand is not converted to desire but is transposed and lived out within the register of desire. This is to say that specific wishes or demands are experienced in conscious and/or unconscious awareness of the lack, and thus the desire that will remain after the gratification of any particular wish or demand is achieved. With this owning, this transposition, this reconciliation, comes a sense of continuity and coherence and even a being at peace in the face of ongoing lack and eventual death.

To own the inherency of lack of unity is to own an absolute of what it is to be human. It is not the negation of a negation but the affirmation of a fundamental negative dimension (loss, lack, finitude, castration, death) of human existence.

Demand constitutes the Other [mother in the place of the Other] as already possessing the "privilege" of satisfying needs, that is to say, the power of depriving them [the needs] of that alone by which they are satisfied [unconditional love as promise of permanent presence]. This privilege of the Other thus outlines the radical form of the gift of that which the Other does not have, namely, its love.

In this way, demand annuls . . . the particularity of everything that

can be granted by transmuting it into a proof of love, and the very satisfactions that it obtains for need are reduced . . . to the level of being
no more than the crushing of the demand for love. . . .

It is necessary, then, that the particularity thus abolished should reappear *beyond* demand. It does, in fact, reappear there, but preserving
the structure contained in the unconditional element of the demand for
love. By a reversal that is not simply a negation of the negation, the power
of pure loss emerges from the residue of an obliteration. For the unconditional element of demand, desire substitutes the "absolute" condition:
this condition unties the knot of that element in the proof of love that is
resistant to the satisfaction of need. Thus desire is neither the appetite
for satisfaction, nor the demand for love, but the difference that results
from the subtraction of the first from the second, the phenomenon of
their splitting. . . .

One can see how the sexual relation occupies this closed field of
desire, in which it will play out its fate. (Lacan, 1977a:286–87)

In owning a want of unity, desire achieves detachment as acknowledged want of being. As want of unity it is there from the
beginning but is covered by demand and cannot be owned as
want of being prior to the differentiation that speech announces.
Where Lacan writes of the "production" or "formation" of desire,
I read him as referring to the gradual process of owning or
assuming one's desire. With the preverbal differentiation that
speech announces, specific wishes and demands can be owned as
"mine," wishes of a subject marked by lack of unity. That would be
one level of owning. The repetition of the preverbal differentiation and loss at the higher oedipal level (symbolic castration, the
assumption of one's gender, finitude, and subjecthood as marked
by lack) allows for a deeper sense of owning and the capacity for
awe more marked by trust than by fear.

Even though difference in conceiving of desire may be large,
I present the above quotations from Lacan in order to show how
much the gist of his thinking about desire could still accord with
an ego psychological concept of desire and of preverbal organization. I now turn to those formulations in Lacan that point to
difference:

1. Lacan conceives of a beyond of the pleasure principle.
2. He repeatedly, though not wholly consistently, places primal repression at the point of language acquisition.
3. The corollary of so locating primal repression is his effort to draw too sharp a line, to my mind, between how the pleasure principle or the laws of language regulate imaging, on the one hand, and how they regulate speech, on the other; thus he draws too sharp a line between how the laws of language structure preverbal differentiations and how they structure those following language acquisition.
4. Above all, the difference hinges on his taking the concept *ego* to refer virtually exclusively to defensive functioning.

I have touched on some of these differences above and will not here elaborate the implications of each. It is my judgment that points 2 and 3 are inconsistent with Lacan's assumption that "It" speaks and also with his interpretation of "the *einziger Zug,* the single stroke, the foundation, the kernel of the ego ideal." The latter, "in so far as the subject clings to it, is in the field of desire, which cannot in any sense be constituted other than in the reign of the signifier, other than at the level in which there is a relation of the subject to the Other. It is the field of the Other that determines the function of the single stroke" (1978a:256).

If my interpretation in chapter 6 of identification with the father of individual prehistory holds, the trust that evolves from such identification is in a different register from that which arises in the dual relationship with the early mother. If so, this "identification" itself would be the kernel or "seed" (Kristeva, 1987b:374) of the ego ideal, and the differentiation of the *einziger Zug* and the identification with the father of individual prehistory that Lacan makes would not hold. Evidently, and notwithstanding his discussion of *being* or *having* the father in *Group Psychology and the Analysis of the Ego* (*Standard Edition,* 18:106), Freud was not locating identification with the father of individual prehistory "in the first field of narcissistic identification," as Lacan asserts

(1978a:256), *nor* was he taking it to be the consequence or outcome of an object-cathexis. Freud wrote:

But whatever the character's later capacity for resisting the influences of abandoned object-cathexis may turn out to be, the effects of the first identifications made in earliest childhood will be general and lasting. This leads us back to the origin of the ego ideal; for behind it there lies hidden an individual's first and most important identification, his identification with the father in his own personal prehistory. This is apparently not in the first instance the consequence or outcome of an object-cathexis; it is a direct and immediate identification and takes place earlier than any object-cathexis. But the object-choices belonging to the first sexual period and relating to the father and mother seem normally to find their outcome in an identification of this kind, and would thus reinforce the primary one. (*Standard Edition*, 19:31)

Lacan's commentary on this passage seems to say that if the identification is prior to the libidinal investment in the mother, it *has* to be narcissistic, and if it isn't, if it is a recognition and modeling mediated at such an early stage by the father, it could only be "a mythical stage, certainly" (1978a:256). What that position does not allow for is the kind of recognition and identification that occurs in the nonperemptory moment. It also does not seem to allow for the idea that the order of the imaginary order is by virtue of the symbolic, by virtue of language in the broad sense that reaches as far back as the first imaging and even, as Lacan asserts elsewhere, to the first organization of perceptual traces.

Defensive, peremptory, or imaginary identification tends to be an in toto type (Smith, 1971:264), motivated by the necessity of disavowing difference. Recognition of difference, recognition of specific traits and also the unity and wholeness of the other is, primitively, allowed for by the nonperemptory moment. This kind of recognition is, of course, of both the mother and father, but the father may be its clearest object for both the boy and the girl, simply because he is other to the symbiotic unity and not the object of peremptory need as is the mother. In chapter 6 I argue that identification with the father of individual prehistory implies unconscious recognition of the system structuring one's existence. All of this is to say that whatever Freud could have meant by identification with the father of individual prehistory, it would begin prior to speech. If we agree with him—and I do— that it is the foundation of the ego ideal, then in some way the preoedipal third terms (that is, delay and other factors that disturb symbiotic tranquility) already have their effect in primitive imaging. "The Other," Lacan wrote, "is already there in the very opening, however evanescent, of the unconscious" (*Séminaire* XI, 1973, as cited by Felman, 1987:22; cf. Lacan, 1978a:130).*

NONDEFENSIVE MOTIVES OF THE EGO

The most important difference between the Lacanian and the ego psychological positions is that Lacan chose to assign to unconscious and conscious ego functioning the purely defensive task of maintaining an achieved false unity and attempting to ward off the undermining of that unity. My assumption that subordinate centers of disequilibrium—realized as unconscious motives to seek out all that has been turned away from—do not forever remain subordinate, together with my assumption that such seeking is a quest of the ego, is a rejection of that Lacanian conceptual strategy.†

*To cite this statement as one of agreement could be thought to ignore the different definitions of repression and the unconscious in Lacan's thinking and in mine. However, the statement holds for Lacan in terms of his definitions and for me in terms of my definitions. I locate unconscious processes as originally present and take repression as beginning with the very first turn away from danger. For Lacan, the unconscious as the discourse of the Other arrives with speech and "the first symbolization of the Oedipal situation" (*Séminaire I*, 100, as cited in Felman, 1987:122).

†I read Lacan's statement, cited above, that in repression "the scansion is alive" (1988b:307) as referring to the subordinate centers of dis-

The reasoning and evidence for those two assumptions is as follows: One aspect of primitive passivity and dependency is to be at the mercy of one's needs and drives, on the one hand, and of the external environment (the presence or absence of the mother) on the other, while having no concept of either internality or externality. Psychically, one automatically takes flight from danger toward the object, also prior to any conceptual organization that would permit categorization of either danger or object. These categorizations take form in the actual fleeing away from and fleeing toward. The question of who or what takes flight also has no definite answer in the mind of the infant. The "I" that is fleeing away from and toward takes form in the process of those psychic activities.

Lacan chose to assign the concept ego to this "I," as did Freud and ego psychology. But during the process of defending against danger, a capacity for primary process orientation is established. This "I" thinks and feels. Furthermore, from the start, as I have suggested above, fleeing from or defending against danger through every mechanism of ego defense implies endopsychic perception of danger. It is dangerous not to keep some eye on danger, and it is this that constitutes the subordinate centers of disequilibrium, even if there can be no initial conceptual categorization of danger. But development is toward the capacity for secondary process, conceptually organized thought. Development is toward the capacity to face the dangers from which one had previously taken flight, to face and mourn losses previously denied, to come into being there where "It" was. Who faces danger, who mourns, and who so comes into being? Is it the same "I" that previously turned away?

This is not to suggest that the concept ego coincides with the unconscious subject of language, but neither does Lacan's concept of subject, at least not that subject huddled up there on the

_____

equilibrium by virtue of which the dynamically repressed is constantly tracked.

left of his Schema R (1977a:197; see also Muller and Richardson, 1982:211, and Green, 1983:165) in the locus of the imaginary, under the sign of the imaginary phallus. The subject, Lacan
wrote, in reference to the earlier Schema L, "is stretched over all
four corners of the Schema" (1977a:194). I exist in an intersubjective world, in a particular cultural embodiment of the symbolic
order. I am that existence, and in so being I am all that to which
the concepts id, ego, ego ideal, and superego refer. The question
of the activities to which those concepts are assigned is purely a
decisional matter of conceptual strategy. I can only say that in
Freud and in America, the concept ego is not assigned to only
defensive functioning.

Lacan is not wholly consistent on this point. There are many
passages in which he writes of the necessity of defense and the
necessity of one's establishing oneself in the imaginary order as
presupposition for entering the symbolic order. Through all his
comments on the defensiveness of the ego there is acknowledgment of only an asymptotic approach to the assumption of one's
desire and subjecthood. This implies the possibility of an assumption by the ego of its subjecthood. Explicitly, Lacan wrote of

the interpretation which moves forward in the direction of the symbolic
structuration of the subject, which is to be located beyond the present
structure of the ego.

Through this we come back to the question of knowing what *Bejahung*,
what assumption by the ego, what *yes* is at issue in the progress of analysis. What *Bejahung* should be elicited, so as to constitute the unveiling
essential to the progress of an analysis? (1988a:65)

The idea of a strong ego invites reification, a tendency to which
Hartmann was especially prone (Smith, 1986a), but also a tendency to which Lacan was not immune. How could he have spent
so much time and energy beating up on the ego if he took it to
be a concept? Partly by way of his own reification, Lacan took the
American idea of a strong ego to mean the establishment of a
more or less impregnable structure of defense against the truth
of human existence. But as I have suggested above in the dis-

cussion of nondefensive unity, one dimension of ego strength is manifested by the capacity to acknowledge danger, loss, finitude, dividedness, and lack, the capacity to listen to the unconscious, to the Other, and to assume one's subjecthood in the light of the Other. Lacan's delineation of modes of defending against these dimensions of life is a contribution to ego psychology. So also is his account of how these acknowledgments come to pass. I learn from him on both scores, but when he writes "the ego" I read "defensive ego functioning."

But do we really need that middle term? All it does, as Schafer has been trying to tell us, is get reified, start fights, and lead people on both sides of the fight to believe they know more than if they talked instead just about "defensive functioning." Or, better, we might talk of just functioning—the situation, the strength of motives and countermotives, all as reasons for disequilibrium leading to a particular position.

Freud said it would be easy to discard conceptual scaffolding. The trouble is, people get turned around and start building on the scaffold's outside. The ego becomes a thing enclosed in a stone wall so thick we may never get it out. Maybe, though, we could just forget it.

CHAPTER FOUR

TRANSFERENCE AND INTERPRETATION

TRANSFERENCE AND LANGUAGE

Transference was first understood as the capacity to misread or distort a new object in terms of prior objects. Analytic experience has taught us to see this first sketch of its meaning as transference in only the narrowest sense. Similarly, analysis conceived as a mode of correcting transference distortions would be an impossibly limited concept of the process of analysis. As mentioned above, the current emphasis is not on transference as a *failure* in reading but on transference as the *power* to read and relate to a new object or situation. It is the power to invest and enter into a relationship or situation in one's own way, in the light of one's prior experience. It is the power to be open to new experience in a way that not only allows the old to affect the new but also allows the new to affect the old.

A "strong misreading" is Harold Bloom's term (1973) for the achievement of a strong reader. A reading is weak to the extent that a text is simply passively understood without the reader's full engagement. To misunderstand or distort a text passively, without engagement, is a weak misreading. A strong reading, exemplified in Bloom by the poet's struggle with a precursor poet, is, by reason of full engagement, bound to be a "misreading." As poet, one brings oneself, with all one's heart and mind, as one is, as one has become through all prior experience, into the en-

counter with the precursor. The product is a changed poet and a
new interpretation of the precursor. Reading, in this sense, and
transference are enactments that change oneself and the text,
object, or world with which one engages. To say that the transference is resistance does not go deep enough. In transference and
resistance, as in Derrida's *différance*, the old resisting the new and
the new resisting the old, deferral and difference are condensed
and played out.

The power of language is by virtue of transference, and the
power of transference is by virtue of language. It is language
and transference together that metonymically carry one along
and metaphorically carry one over,* as one is, toward the new and
toward change.

The turning away from the original state of unmet neediness
toward an image of the object I have defined as primal repression. Turning from wishes that signal danger subsequent to preconscious organization, as I shall discuss, is repression proper.
Turning away from external danger is denial and disavowal.

What is unconscious is all that one has turned away from
together with the "mechanism" of the turning itself. However,
whatever one has turned away from is marked as a danger to be
faced or a loss to be mourned. Whatever has been turned away
from in this sense speaks, in such fashion, depending on how
one is, to drive one away as from danger or to call one back as to
one's origin. I have repeatedly stressed Freud's dictum that the
direction of development is toward being able to turn and face
danger in an exercise of judgment rather than having to resort
to automatic flight or fight.

In the perpetual interplay of these turnings, the greater the
differentiation and integration achieved, the greater the capacity
to face danger. The greater the capacity to face danger, including the danger of lack of unity that is forever at the heart of the

---

*Laplanche (1976:138) wrote, "'Transference,' 'metaphor': the word
is the same, and it originally means 'carrying over'."

self, the greater the capacity also to turn toward, recognize and love the object.

These turnings are the structure of transference as a universal. In the psychoanalytic situation, transference is the enactment—the coming to language—between analysand and analyst of these turnings. The analysand's "transference" and the analyst's "countertransference" are simply terms that designate whether the source of transference is in the analysand or the analyst. What is called the therapeutic alliance is, in these terms, the centerpiece of both the analysand's and the analyst's transference.

Language allows for the analysand's multiple conscious and unconscious narratives, and transference brings these narratives alive in the relationship between analysand and analyst. The analyst's own narratives are held in abeyance, not only to leave room for the overt utterance of those of the analysand but also to leave room for the analyst to be, in some sense, those figures that he or she is seen to be in the analysand's stories. I don't mean playacting or assuming a role. I mean that those elements in the analyst's experience that in some way match the important figures in the analysand's conscious and unconscious stories come to the fore, often before the analyst knows it, and to that extent, he or she *is* those figures. The analyst's desire becomes, in some degree, the desire of important figures in the analysand's story.* This is one way in which the analyst comes to know the analysand and his or her story. For both analyst and analysand, these are transference stories. In some measure, each enters the other's story.

In a discussion of Winnicott's concept of transitional objects, Fox wrote:

*I suggest that "The Two Analyses of Mr. Z" (Kohut, 1979) is not only the story of a changed theoretical stance of Kohut's in the direction of Lacan (see Muller, 1989) but also the evocation of desire of the analysand's mother in the first analysis and of his father in the second. No doubt this would have occurred in some measure quite aside from the analyst's theoretical position.

Transference as it occurs in the clinical situation is such an intermediate experience, an illusion intermediate between full object relating and complete narcissistic retreat. It is not merely a displacement of past figures on to the blank screen of the analyst but a finding of these fantasied figures in the person of the other. Just as the dream involves more than a distorted recreation of an unconscious wish, the transference requires that bit of reality (or day residue) which lends itself to representability. (1984:233)

Transference overtly reveals who the analysand is, and transference covertly reveals who the analyst is. While largely silent, the analyst comes to be known. There are the questions asked, the interpretations given, the intonation and timing of "hm's," the qualities of silence, the eloquence or lack thereof of gestures, movement or stillness, and even minimal responses to humor, humiliation, grief, depression, panic, rage, envy, hate, elation, sorrow, sexual desire, and love. Often the analysand's protests regarding the analyst's anonymity (and also the analyst's silent reflections about the analysand's distorted picture of the analyst) arise as a defense against the astonishing intimacy of the knowledge each comes to have of the other.

Correcting distortions, explaining distortions, was more or less what Freud tried with Dora. It was in the wake of that colossal failure, though not without later lapses, that he came to realize that what is of central value comes to pass by way of transference. Unconscious narratives come to light where the analyst is willing and able to enter the story.

Is the aim of all this, then, to make the unconscious conscious? What, anyway, does it mean to say, "where id was there ego shall be" (*Standard Edition*, 22:80)? Loewald's reading is "where id was ego shall come into being." For him, Freud's meaning (and also Heidegger's thinking on *Geworfenheit*, thrownness, and *Entwerfen*, project) is epitomized "in the dictum: Become what you are" (1978:19).

To the extent to which the individual remains entangled in his unappropriated id or disowns it, as in repression—and most of us do to a considerable extent—he is driven by unmastered unconscious forces within himself. He is free to develop, to engender his future, to the extent to which he remains or becomes open to his id and can personalize, again and again and on various levels, his unconscious powers. For Freud these unconscious powers are the true psychic reality. This apersonal ground of our existence, he claims, we are called upon to make human, to make, each in his own way, into a person. (Loewald, 1978:25)

He also wrote:

The id or dynamic unconscious . . . is the past history of the individual in the sense of being a mode of experience or mentation that is older than those forms of mental processes we are familiar with from conscious, rational life. . . .

This "archaic" mode of mentation, however, is also a newly rediscovered and appreciated mode that is asserting its own validity and power in our culture. The discoveries, the thrust of psychoanalysis—almost against the conscious intentions of its creator—have contributed an important share to the new valuation of the irrational unconscious. In modern art, literature, and philosophy; in the mood, aspirations, conduct of life of the younger generation, we see a fresh flowering of the more ancient, more deeply rooted mode of human experience which perhaps is leading toward a less rigid, less frozen, and more humane rationality. Freud called the dynamic unconscious indestructible in comparison with the ephemeral and fragile, but infinitely precious, formations of consciousness. Where id was, there ego shall come into being. Too easily and too often ego is equated with rigid, unmodulated, and unyielding rationality. So today we are moved to add: where ego is, there id shall come into being again to renew the life of the ego and of reason. (pp. 15–16)

The question of the goal of analysis is, perhaps, the ultimate instance of handing the analysand's question—the analysand's ultimate question—back to the analysand. The analyst, the one who is supposed to know, does not know who the analysand should or will come to be. This is the core of the analyst's abstinence. That abstinence is finally revealed to be not a holding back of knowledge on the part of the analyst, but an absence, a lack of knowledge. The analyst's silence here is a steadfast refusal to cover lack of knowledge with glib, empty speech; it is to refrain from substituting the analyst's decisions or values where those of the analysand are called for.

The work of the analyst is to facilitate the analysand's achieving the means of being, the means of exercising his or her own freedom. The analyst interprets defenses and resistances against that which, in the psychic reality of the analysand, is perceived as danger. In the realm of the analysand's psychic reality, all dangers are real dangers. However, when a change in defensive posture occurs through interpretations informed by the analyst having entered the analysand's story, dangers heretofore avoided can be faced and sometimes dispelled. Dispelling danger, though, may not be a matter for joy. To do away with lesser dangers often brings into view more serious threats that cannot be dispelled.

Ultimately, however, the coming to light of unconscious narratives allows for the construction of a fuller story of one's life, which is to say it allows for a fuller life. The wider scope of memory and of present awareness also means a more open, less defended stance toward one's future. But it is not enough to characterize transference reenactment as simply the coming to life and language of the analysand's narratives or, in Lacan's terms, the enactment of the reality of the unconscious. It *is* that, but the narratives come alive by virtue of the replaying of those interactions through which the narratives were originally constructed.

I take the preceding discussion to be a general statement of widely held views of transference. While not engaging all his pertinent concepts (and modifying some of those I do engage), I turn now to an exposition of how this understanding of transference is both specified and elaborated in the thought of Lacan.

TRANSFERENCE AND THE LANGUAGE OF LACAN

In approaching what I consider both new and good in Lacan's thought on transference, I should mention that sometimes the struggle to understand him results in the discovery that

he is telling us what we already know. Analysis is not limited to
relieving symptoms. It is not just a matter of making the contents
of the dynamically repressed conscious. It is not a dual relationship between one conscious mind and another but a situation
informed by the unconscious of both the analysand and the analyst. Transference, positive transference, is love, but the analyst
realizes that within or beyond the wish for love is the more fundamental desire for recognition. In the acknowledgment of desire
as indestructible want of being, desire and subjecthood are assumed and the transference is resolved.

That much of this we already knew (whether or not we exactly
knew we knew it) is not so surprising in view of Lacan's claim that
his teaching was, centrally, a return to Freud. He did not present
many of his ideas as being of his own devising. He instead cried
out to analysts of his day that they had forgotten the fundamen-
tals. Those of us who entered the field at about the time he was
giving utterance to what we now have in English as *Ecrits* and *The
Four Fundamental Concepts of Psycho-Analysis* can recognize criti-
cisms that we also held or that were in the air at the time. How else
would Sullivan, Winnicott, and Kohut have become the heroes
of so many? Rapaport, Loewald, and Schafer have consistently
addressed or offered alternatives to the narrow, pseudoexplanatory psychoanalytic formulations appearing under the guise of
orthodoxy. But, as I shall discuss in chapter 6, no group is immune to blind, follow-the-leader orthodoxy. I believe that Lacan,
in his late years, worried about just that among Lacanians.

The call for a return to Freud appears in Lacan's discussions
of transference. What is commonly accepted as new or—if he is
right in saying it was already there in Freud—newly explicated
is Lacan's idea that the unconscious is structured like a language.
Also particular with Lacan, and in line with that idea, is his way of
describing the want of being that brings the subject to treatment
in terms of the want of being with which the subject entered the
world, meaning the linguistically constituted world.

Lacan sees such want of being as manifested by desire already

there within the infant's demands. The lack is inscribed by primal repression at the point of entrance into language. However,
as I have stressed, it is not always clear when Lacan refers to language (and entry into language) whether he means the laws of
language that structure the subject from the beginning—including the subject in its primitive imaging—or those laws as they
become manifest in speech as such; nor is it clear whether he
means entry into language as entry, at a higher level, into the
symbolic order by virtue of submitting to those laws (the Law) in
the resolution of the oedipal phase. It is not always clear, that is,
whether he refers to language or to the effects of the laws of language at a certain era of development. To phrase it alternately,
it is often uncertain whether he means, in a particular passage,
language as a system (*la langue*) or language as speech (*la parole*),
language competence or language performance. Regarding the
latter, it is my opinion that the lack of clarity is intended—he
wanted to mean both. "It," the Other, speaks. Language and the
laws of language were there before the subject came into being
and remain as the medium in which it comes to recognize its own
lack and limit.

Lacan wrote of the position of the analyst as "in the place of
the Other" and as the one who is "supposed to know," the latter
especially in those texts in which he specifically addressed transference. Although the analyst does not take himself or herself
as the authority who is "supposed to know," this way of thinking
about the analyst does become the transference wish and assumption of the analysand. "There is transference," Lacan wrote, "as
soon as there is a subject who is supposed to know" (1978a:230).

In the resolution of the transference the analysand is able to
assume his or her subjecthood as marked by lack, by recognizing
the lack in the one who is supposed to know, the one in the place
of the Other, the lack in the Other (Lacan, 1977a:263). That is,
neither the one in the place of the Other nor the Other (the laws
of language that structure one's being) can erase the want-to-be,
the want of being, that is constitutive of human being. But the ini-

tial attribution to the analysand of desire directed toward the one who is supposed to know seems a bit cerebral, a bit off the mark of being that which the analysand would even dimly conceive as the answer to his or her want of being. To my way of thinking, "desire as the nodal phenomenon of the human being" (1978a:231) fits better with thinking of transference in terms of the analyst in the place of the Other. It better accords with how the infant, too young to know or care about knowledge, enters the world. It also accords with Lacan's emphasis on the mother and father being in the place of the Other not because they have superior knowledge (cf. Lacan, 1977a:174) but because they represent the future and a nonnarcissistic way of being in the world.

Primarily, the Other (with the capital O) designates law and language. The other use of the Other is in reference to an object in the place of the Other, that is, who represents (Lacan, 1977a:264) the Other and is mediator of language, law, and the symbolic order as embodied in a particular culture. In the second sense, to the extent the other is an object of demand on the model of original wishes representing the satisfaction of physical needs it is other (with a small o); to the extent the other is the object of desire (that is, wanting that manifests a lack or want of being inherent in the subject as subject), it is Other in the sense of being in the place of the Other. The corollary is that "desire presupposes the symbolic order" (Muller and Richardson, 1982:413).

TRACES, IMAGES, AND IMAGINARY COMPETENCE

The lack marking the subject is a consequence of having been diverted from the real into imagery and language. Regarding the diversion in which the original hallucinatory image is falsely substituted for the mother, Freud emphasizes the "correction" brought about by the identity of thought that allows for the recognition of the mother as such. Lacan, on the other hand, stresses that once diverted into language, there is no going back. The only way of knowing the mother as such is a matter of how the laws of language structure the capacity for the identity of thought. That way of being in the world is accompanied by a sense of loss of a prior, actual or imagined, different engagement with the mother as real. Freud's emphasis is on the means of refinding the object; Lacan's is on the permanent mark of lack the subject carries into that refinding.

I take imaginary competence not only as referring to an unconscious structured like a language even prior to speech—a structuring that allows for speech—but also as referring to the organization of self and world that is vastly extended in the domain of relatedness, primarily dual, from the time of speech acquisition to the triadic oedipal resolution. I say primarily dual because third terms are (the Other is) around from the beginning, all grouped by Freud under that great mythical name, the father of individual prehistory, to be discussed in chapter 6.

If primitive imaging seems too early a point to bring in Lacan's ideas (and according to him, Freud's) on the structuring functions of language and on the image as signifier, we should note that Lacan went even earlier, calling the perceptual traces "signifiers" (1978a:46). And, if it seems too removed from the topic of transference, we should remember that his discussion of the "irreducible signifier," the "originally repressed signifier," and the "necessity of that moment in which the subject as X can be constituted only from the *Urverdrängung*, from the necessary fall of this first signifier," is to be found in the chapter "From Interpretation to the Transference" in the *Four Principles*.

Regarding perceptual traces and Freud's optical schema wherein the psychical appears as the virtual, Lacan wrote:

> This is the locus where the affair of the subject of the unconscious is played out . . . as an immense display, a special spectre, situated between perception and consciousness. . . . [T]he interval that separates them, in which the place of the Other is situated, [is the interval] in which the subject is constituted.
>
> How do the *Wahrnehmungszeichen*, the traces of perception, function? Freud . . . designates a time when these *Wahrnehmungszeichen* must be

constituted in simultaneity. What is this time, if not signifying synchrony?
And, of course, Freud says this all the more in that he does not know
that he is saying it fifty years before the linguists. But we can immediately give to the *Wahrnehmungszeichen* their true name of *signifiers*. . . .
Freud, when he comes back to this locus in *The Interpretation of Dreams*,
designates still other layers, in which the traces are constituted this time
by analogy. What we have here are those functions of contrast and simili-
tude so essential in the constitution of metaphor, which is introduced by
a diachrony. . . .

We find in Freud's articulations a quite unambiguous indication that
what is involved in this synchrony is not only a network formed by random and contiguous associations. The signifiers were able to constitute
themselves in simultaneity only by virtue of a very defined structure of
constituent diachrony. (1978a:45–46)

The passage in "From Interpretation to the Transference"
about an "irreducible signifier," the "originally repressed signifier," moves from perceptual traces to images. I read, interpret,
extrapolate, or alter it as follows: The irreducible, originally repressed signifier is not the first hallucinatory image of the object.
That first image arises at a moment of peremptory need as a
memory and an anticipation of the experience of satisfaction.
What is turned away from in the identity of thought is not the
image of the object but the image *as* hallucination, which quickly
comes to be associated with the danger it attempts to avert. Because of the system constituted by need, absence of the object
of need, and the primary autonomous capacities of perception,
ideation, affect, memory, and anticipation, such an image as signifier signifies the experience of satisfaction. But there is no way
that the infant can "know" that, even unconsciously, if we assume
a progressive organization of unconscious knowledge. So far as
the infant is concerned, the original image is just as much "kernel,
a *kern*, to use Freud's own term, of *non-sense*" (Lacan, 1978a:250)
as is the subsequently established "originally repressed signifier."
However, the image of the experience of satisfaction comes to
be more danger-distant, comes to have meaning, comes to be a

signifier whose signified and referent are known, as primary process thinking achieves progressive organization along the lines of Freud's description of the organization of the perceptual traces.

The image of the mother arising at a moment of peremptory need has to do with the satisfaction of physical need. It is the original demand. I would suggest that the similarly irreducible signifier fated for repression arises in the nonperemptory moment, when needs are not urgent and imagery arises from more varied foci of disequilibrium. These, too, representatives of the anlagen of desire, would initially be without sense. However, this more free and neutral imaging would be the route through which a world of imagery opens up, in which meaning comes to be, and in which the subject accomplishes its initial recognition of itself as subject.

This recognition arrives as catastrophe and loss. The senseless signifier that is the closest harbinger of such awareness of separateness becomes the originally repressed signifier. Subsequent signifiers associated with it will also be repressed. But the repression of such a series of signifiers, the last functioning as a screen for the prior ones, can be taken as a form of denial or negation that is a first step in the acknowledgment of one's subjecthood. The initial denial and loss of one's subjecthood is thus how one's subjecthood is constituted. One's subjecthood is first encountered as the danger of separateness and, by virtue of that loss and by virtue of the non-sense of the signifiers of that stage, nothingness. But, as one's subjecthood, it comes to be viewed as an especially precious and, thereby, enigmatic and uncanny danger. It is not just a danger to be faced but a danger to be assumed.

Barring severe developmental defect or massive defense, as in Melanie Klein's patient mentioned above (a patient Lacan refers to as having language but not speech), speech announces a unity achieved, a brush with the first signifier of one's subjecthood already encountered, and indicates that the capacity for repression proper has been established. What Lacan usually means by primal repression is the repression of the first signifier of one's subjecthood—a turning away from difference, from the third term, from the Other, a turning from the Other in which, by negation, the Other is acknowledged and the unconscious subject is constituted. That usage renders his concept of primal repression a borderline one, leaving uncertain whether he refers to the first instance of repression proper or the last and most crucial instance of primal repression—the instance wherein the subject's concern about its subjecthood has come into play and is repressed.

I have emphasized that the imaginary in the preoedipal era is a means of achieving a degree of unity, primarily in the dual mode of relating. Such unity is the presupposition for entering the oedipal era. It is only defensive if beyond its time. Lacan speaks of the "formative effects" (1977a:3) of the mirror stage and in other passages (for example, 1977a:4, 5, 17, 89, 120, 308; 1978a:144)* variously defends the importance of imaginary competence. Even in *his* definition of the ego, if there is no ego there, there is no there there. He wrote: "The only object that is within the analyst's reach is the imaginary relation that links him to the subject *qua* ego" (1977a:45). And also:

> In order to know how to reply to the subject in analysis, the procedure is to recognize first of all the place where his *ego* is, the *ego* that Freud himself defined as an *ego* formed of verbal nucleus; in other words, to know through whom and for whom the subject poses *his question*. So long as this is not known, there will be the risk of a misunderstanding concerning the desire that is there to be recognized and concerning the object to whom this desire is addressed. (1977a:89)

Lacan spoke in his first seminar about Melanie Klein's utterly indifferent and "absent" four-year-old patient as a subject in whom "there is no unconscious whatever," no capacity to "put

---

*Muller and Richardson (1982:403) comment on one of these passages: "The structuring of the imaginary order appears quite necessary before full entrance into the symbolic order is possible." Lacan's phrasing is "The subject . . . has to . . . constitute himself in his imaginary reality" (1978a:144).

into play the imaginary and the real, and thus conquer his development" (*Séminaire* I, 1975:100, as cited in Felman, 1987:122). "What does not happen," he said, "is the free play, the conjunction between the different forms—the real and the imaginary—of the objects" (Felman, p. 111). "Speech and language are not the same; this child is . . . master of language, but he does not speak. It is a subject who is there and who, literally, does not answer. Speech has not come to him, the Real and the Imaginary are the same" (p. 113).

I take "no unconscious" to mean no "originally repressed signifier" of lack and loss from which desire and an appeal or call to the other could originate; Lacan's assumption, then, is that nothing in this extremely apathetic child's life had come alive to the point that a signifier would be repressed by reason of having intimated separate subjecthood.

What has all this to do with Lacan's thought about transference and interpretation? In his thinking it is this: everything pertaining to one's desire and subjecthood that has been crucially denied or hidden in the demand for love must be recognized, brought to light. And the recognition, the interpretation, must be of the particular signifiers repressed by a particular subject.

> Interpretation is a signification that is not just any signification. . . . It has the effect of bringing out an irreducible signifier. . . . What is there is rich and complex, when it is a question of the unconscious of the subject, and intended to bring out irreducible, *non-sensical*—composed of non-meanings—signifying elements. . . .
> Interpretation is not open to all meanings. It is not just any interpretation. It is significant interpretation, one that must not be missed. This does not mean that it is not this signification that is essential to the advent of the subject. What is essential is that he should see, beyond this signification, to what signifier—to what irreducible, traumatic, non-meaning—he is, as a subject, subjected. (1978a:250–51; see also p. 276)

This is an ultimate formulation of thrownness. What Lacan talks about here is bedrock—bedrock beyond its manifestations in the form of castration anxiety and penis envy. It is a hard

goal. I would judge that the bringing to light of even the last in
the primitive series of representatives of the originally repressed
signifier is partly a matter of luck. Most reconstructions—efficacious enough, I believe—are of the situation that originally
evoked such a series of signifiers, as that comes to light in the
transference recapitulation. But, of course, efficacious interpretations and reconstructions so established will be current links in
the original signifying chain, whether or not the original links of
non-meaning come to light. No doubt some close representatives
of those original links have appeared in a successful analysis, even
if unnoticed by analyst or analysand. Not everything gets interpreted. And, even if it could be, the point is that beyond signification, beyond meaning, it is essential to come to the nothingness
at the core—a nothingness sustained by language, by the Other.

CHAPTER FIVE

THE SIGNIFYING ROLE OF AFFECT

I am convinced—or in any event willing, I think, to be convinced—that the more the originally repressed signifiers are brought to light, the more efficacious the experience of analysis becomes. However, the relinquishment of ego defenses in an asymptotic approach to dimensions of subjecthood originally repressed, or yet to be achieved, may not be manifested by arriving beyond the "signification that is essential to the advent of the subject . . . to [the] signifier—to [the] irreducible, traumatic, non-meaning—[to which] he is, as a subject, subjected" (Lacan, 1978a:250–51). Although the analysand might be brought to the point of such response by pertinent significant interpretations, his or her basic sense of thrownness into the world might be manifested by an affective equivalent of such bedrock experience.

Before the throwing up of all Lacanian hands at even the mention of affect, we might pause to consider how it is that affect also is a part of the signifying system.

If we could break the Lacanian barrier against thinking of the concept ego as assigned to *any* nondefensive functioning, we could lapse back into the familiar Freudian phrasing of the ego as the seat of the emotions. Perhaps Lacan had so little (at least conceptually) to do with the emotions in part to avoid such a lapse. But let us not even try to break that barrier here. Let us just talk about affective response and, to prepare the way for that, again about the pleasure principle.

AFFIRMATION AND NEGATION

To set the scene in which, like Kristeva (1983) and Green (1983), I attempt to introduce affect into Lacan—no, not introduce, but show where it is already there, hidden in the open—I would like to emphasize again that need or drive, affectively and ideationally represented, together with the absence of the object of need and with the pertinent innate capacities, constitutes a system. How that system works is what the statement of the pleasure principle specifies. The pleasure principle is essentially coterminous with psychic determinism, overdetermination, and the principle of multiple function (Waelder, 1936). At every level of psychic organization, at every level of maturity, each focus of disequilibrium (together with the affective context, memory and anticipation, and the structural conditions that guide and constrain the resolution of disequilibrium) has its impact and effectiveness. This effectiveness would hold not only for the macroscopic directionality or intentionality of behavior but also for the microscopic selection of each instance of metonymic elaboration or metaphoric condensation occurring in the carrying out of that resolution. This is the meaning of Lacan's (and implicitly Freud's) statement, "The signifiers were able to constitute themselves in simultaneity only by virtue of a very defined structure of constituent diachrony" (1978a:46).

The directionality of primitive mentation (which precedes the intentionality allowed by the changed structural conditions of linguistically based, secondary process thought) is the turning away from a center of disequilibrium (in George Klein's thought, from an area of imbalance [1967]) toward an object that might afford resolution of that disequilibrium. Although the dynamic of motivation is from high tension to low, there could be no tension without structure, that is, tension maintenance. Learning amounts to the establishment of new-order tension-maintaining structures. The direction of overall development is thus toward higher tension tolerance—as, for example, in turning to face danger rather than immediately discharging tension in automatic fight or flight responses (Freud, *Standard Edition*, 12:221; Rapaport, 1960:875–77, 890).

The pleasure principle is (like the laws of language) a statement of how the system works. It is true that often the conscious response to disequilibrium, especially primitively, is affective unpleasure, as manifested in the cry to which the mother responds. And that is where the principle got its first name—the unpleasure principle. However, the principle is simply a statement of how things work, and things work in accord with it whether or not there is conscious experience of pleasure or unpleasure (see Rapaport, 1960:875–77; 1953:504; Rapaport and Gill, 1959:802; Smith, 1977).

With development, and even from the start in nonperemptory imaging and feeling, not every focus of disequilibrium signals danger and thus affective unpleasure. The foci of nondangerous disequilibrium motivate in the adult, for instance, not only sexual union but also the following out of one's interests and projects. When the reality principle comes into play, and even when the repetition compulsion comes into play, it is still a matter of foci of disequilibrium motivating a turn toward objects that promise resolution of disequilibrium, but under awesomely more complex structural conditions.

Let us leave the infant and look at Freud's account of a high-level instance of the binarism Lacan spoke of as one way in which the laws of language have their effects:

> The study of judgement affords us, perhaps for the first time, an insight into the origin of an intellectual function from the interplay of the primary instinctual impulses. Judging is a continuation, along the lines of expediency, of the original process by which the ego took things into itself or expelled them from itself, according to the pleasure principle. The polarity of judgement appears to correspond to the opposition of

the two groups of instincts which we have supposed to exist. Affirmation—as a substitute for uniting—belongs to Eros; negation—the successor to expulsion—belongs to the instinct of destruction. (*Standard Edition*, 19:239)

Both Freud and Lacan held that a beyond of the pleasure principle exists. They held such a position because each was enmeshed in the usage according to which the pleasure principle was limited to primitive primary process thinking, or was a principle of pleasure seeking, or both. Indeed, the above passage is shortly followed by a remark about "freedom from . . . the compulsion of the pleasure principle." But what was importantly problematized in *Beyond the Pleasure Principle* and in Lacan's (and Derrida's [1987]) attention to that text was precisely this narrow usage of the pleasure principle. In the negative therapeutic reaction and the repetition compulsion Freud encountered structural conditions for which no simplistic deployment of a theory of wish-fulfillment could account.

The point of the Freudian passage is not only that it presents the operation of the pleasure principle in a way that is virtually synonymous with the way Lacan situates binarism in the laws of language, but also that it is a reference to the operation of the pleasure principle at a very advanced level. The subsequent reference to freedom from the compulsion of the pleasure principle is a reference to primitive experience, prior to the development and organization of higher-level structures that provide the capacity for judgment and, in general, for a relative degree of autonomy from compulsion—that is, it is a reference to freedom from being at the mercy of either the drives or the external environment (Rapaport, 1957).

If the pleasure principle not only includes but also goes beyond the turn from danger signaled by conscious unpleasure to the object that promises resolution of that danger, what, then, is the place of the signifying role of affect? Is affect, as such, as Green (1983) suggests, to be taken as a signifier?

AFFECT AND SIGNIFICATION

To say that pleasure and unpleasure as such have nothing to do with the pleasure principle* is not to say that affective experience has no signifying role along with ideation and thought. The role of affect in relation to the pleasure principle can be understood in perfect analogy with Freud's final statement on the relation between speech and the preconscious organization (*Standard Edition*, 23:162), in which Freud took the preverbal accomplishment of the preconscious organization to be the structural achievement that allows for speech. The presence of speech is, then, a sure sign that preconscious organization has been accomplished.

While the model for explaining the pleasure principle has been that of the anxiety signal as a response to danger, danger is— and with development progressively becomes—only one class of foci of disequilibrium. But even in the case of unconscious scansion that reveals a potential danger situation, one would have to assume that the unconscious system usually works to turn away from that situation prior to the evocation of even an anxiety signal. However, if anxiety is evoked, it is a sure sign that a danger situation, even though not known consciously, has been encountered. Only on the basis of that understanding can we reclaim and reestablish everything Freud wrote about the signifying role of affect.

The trouble with Green's idea that affect should be taken as a second-order signifier is that signifiers can be repressed and affect cannot. Freud dismissed the claim that unconscious thinking was a contradiction in terms, but he consistently maintained that unconscious affect *was* such a contradiction (Freud, *Standard Edition*, 14:177–78, 19:22–23, 21:135). When we speak, as

---

*The pleasure principle, Rapaport said, "has not *per se* anything to do with pleasure or pain" (1957–59, 1:74).

everyone does, of unconscious anxiety, rage, or desire, what we mean, or what we ought to mean, is that certain ideas—a certain train of thought or chain of signifiers—are repressed that, if de-repressed, would be accompanied by the said affects. The affects themselves are not repressed, nor does repression occur to avoid the affects.

Freud wrote: "It might be said that symptoms are created so as to avoid the generating of anxiety. But this does not go deep enough. It would be truer to say that symptoms are created so as to avoid a *danger-situation* whose presence has been signalled by the generation of anxiety" (*Standard Edition*, 20:129). This statement served to correct the earlier one in "The Unconscious," where he wrote, "to suppress the development of affect is the true aim of repression and . . . its work is incomplete if this aim is not achieved" (*Standard Edition*, 14:178). But even there, he was not harboring a concept of unconscious affect. The translation in the *Collected Papers* is unambiguous:

We apply the term "unconscious" to those affects that are restored when we undo the work of repression. So . . . the use of the [term] . . . is logical; but a comparison of the unconscious affect with the unconscious idea reveals the significant difference that the unconscious idea continues, after repression, as an actual formation in the system *Ucs*, whilst to the unconscious affect there corresponds in the same system only a potential disposition which is prevented from developing further. (1915d:110–11)

This might seem like quibbling. But what is at stake, in my opinion, is this: Freud's statement that the quality of being conscious or not represents our one beacon light is a statement of dependency on consciousness and on consciousness having a matrix that can exist in no other form than a conscious one. That matrix is affect. Rapaport's (1953) tentative attempt to picture a progressive structuralization of affect as such (p. 493), of defense against affect (p. 491), and of unconscious affect (p. 496), and, in general, to present the structural view of affect as "going beyond" Freud's careful statement of only an unconscious potential disposition led Schur (1953) down the wrong road (see Smith, 1970). It is a road that Green, with his concept of affect as signifiers capable of repression, has discovered on his own.

How is it, then, that affect as at least sometimes the conscious indicator of the workings of the pleasure principle "provides the thought-process with its most important clues" (Freud, 1900a:536; cf. *Standard Edition*, 5:602)?

I have maintained (1970) that affect as an always conscious, *de novo* response is the structural view of affect that accords with Freud's view of affect from the time of *Inhibitions, Symptoms, and Anxiety* (1926). It is a structural view of affect that avoids the Rapaport/Schur/Green fallacy of taking affect to be structure or as capable of becoming structuralized and therefore capable of unconscious existence. (For a similar view of affect as only conscious see Lacan, 1978a:217; 1978b:78–97; and Muller and Richardson, 1982:139.) *De novo* would not carry the meaning of "*de novo* in repression," Freud's earlier term when he took anxiety as arising from the conversion of libido that had been repressed. *De novo* means simply conscious immediate response to inner and outer events, conditioned by memory and anticipation. This is to say, the more complex and nuanced one's memory, anticipation, and thought, the more complex and nuanced one's affective responses will be.

AFFECTIVE RECOGNITION

Let us return to the idea of the ongoing, unconscious scansion of inner and outer worlds. Recall that "It" reads (Lacan, *Séminaire* XX, 1975:38, as cited by Felman, 1987:22) and that for Lacan "It" is the Other, a reading by virtue of the unconscious laws of language. I believe an equally valid phrasing that would in no way subvert Lacan's concept of the unconscious as the discourse of the Other (1977a:312) is that the reading is by the unconscious ego in accord with the pleasure principle—the pleasure principle not just in the mode of the primitive massive move from dominant disequilibrium toward the object, but also in the mode of following out those subordinate centers of disequilibrium that motivate a refinding of all that has been turned away from. But let us not engage "the Other"/"unconscious ego" difference beyond simply marking the question of whether one or both concepts might prove advantageous for illuminating the signifying role of affect.

Every step in the ongoing scansion that evokes *any* conscious response would be marked by conscious affective response. One's basic conscious attunement to inner and outer worlds is thus mediated by affect and is lived out as one's dominant mood. However, if affect existed in isolation, impossible anyway since it is the response *of* the subject *to* something, there would be no attunement. This could be taken as one reason for Lacan's inattention to affect. Affect as conscious response never occurs except as affective context for ideation or thought, that is, a signifier or signifying chain. That to which affect is a response can only come to light by passing through the defiles of the chain of signifiers. What is responded to might be a repressed signifier that remains repressed. But *some* conscious signifiers representing the repressed would appear in the context of affective response. Perhaps the chain of signifiers appearing would negate those that remained repressed. In such a case one could say that the affective response as such is more true to what the unconscious scanning has glimpsed than are the negating conscious signifiers of which it is the context. In that sense there would be warrant for saying that affective recognition exceeds that of conscious thought. "*The ideational material has undergone displacements and substitutions, whereas the affects have remained unchanged.* It is small wonder that the ideational material, which has been changed by dream-distortion, should no longer be compatible with the affect, which is retained unmodified" (Freud, *Standard Edition*, 5:460–61).

The same principle obtains in the original form of the idea and the affect as representatives of the drive. The affect is "true" to the disequilibrium or imbalance that is the source of the drive. The idea as an image of fulfillment could be said to cover or falsify lack, or at least to affirm it only in the mode of negating it.

Of course, "affective recognition" is also a shorthand way of talking about any real recognition as opposed to some intellectualized, relatively affectless, obsessional chain of signifiers. When "affective recognition," though, is used in reference to an instance of vivid affective response, true to an unconscious tendency that its accompanying chain of conscious signifiers negates, the recognition that is structured and enters the concatenation of the signifier, the recognition that has a chance of leading to full recognition, is recognition by negation. This, I take it, was Lacan's central reason for attending the signifiers and letting the affect take care of itself. Which, one should add, it always does. That affect has no explicit place in his theory of the signifier does not mean that Lacan did not follow the clues of his own and his analysand's affective responses, nor count them at times, as I attempt to show in my conclusion, as the primary way of signifying insight achieved. As Lacan's reference to "signifying synchrony" (1978a:46) would suggest, not everything that signifies is a signifier in the sense of Freud's ideation and thought.

The pleasure principle in the narrow sense of referring only to primary process functioning and the reality principle as the mode of regulation of secondary process functioning were crucial to Freud's effort to conceptualize the differences between primitive and advanced functioning. Sixty years later, Lacan believed that that emphasis on difference, especially in ego psychology, had lost touch with the elements of sameness in primitive and advanced functioning and thus with the real life of Freud's discoveries. Much in his way of elaborating the thesis that the unconscious is structured like a language was an effort to reestablish that sameness. I believe that Loewald, at approximately the same time, began in his own very different way to devote himself to the same task. Rapaport's effort to emphasize the pleasure principle in the broad sense (what I referred to in my 1977 article as "the

Pleasure Principle") as the same principle regardless of apparent variations introduced by structural conditions or level of development is, I believe, in line with this dimension of Lacan's and Loewald's projects.

I have attempted above to divorce the pleasure principle from the idea of pleasure seeking, to show the pleasure principle as a universal, unconscious mode of regulation in the sense of being a statement of how things work, and to justify Freud's insistence that affect is limited to conscious ego response. I do not consider affect in terms of discharge, because I believe that to stress affect as conscious ego response represents better its signifying role. Although Freud was given to overemphasizing the economic and also to talking of the ego as "producing" or "reproducing" affect rather than referring to affect as ego response, the latter is more in line with the gist of *Inhibitions, Symptoms, and Anxiety*:

> How is it possible, from an economic point of view, for a mere process of withdrawal and discharge, like the withdrawal of a preconscious ego-cathexis, to produce unpleasure and anxiety, seeing that, according to our assumptions, unpleasure and anxiety can only arise as a result of an *increase* in cathexis? The reply is that this causal sequence should not be explained from an economic point of view. Anxiety is not newly created in repression; it is reproduced as an affective state in accordance with an already existing mnemic image. (*Standard Edition*, 20:93)

Unconscious dangers or foci of disequilibrium are marked as such by virtue of the linguistic organization of the unconscious, which unconscious ego scansion detects, and not by an unconscious affect charge. The pleasure principle is guided by those markings rather than by affect as such. The establishment of these points allows a signifying function for conscious affective experience on the same level as conscious verbal thought and speech.

> Signal affect . . . is the correlate of highly differentiated . . . active ego functioning. Thus affect signals as modulated ego responses occur on the basis of anticipation, recall, or in a [currently perceived] situation. How-

ever, it is not affect as a quantitative factor which is modulated. Rather, signal affective responses occur in situations (and ego states) which permit simultaneous attention to multiple stimuli, none of them compelling immediate or total response.

Finally, [a] general theory of affect would not limit the affective response of active ego functioning to signal affect. Extremes of affective response occur not only passively as in affect storms or overwhelming trauma, but also as active affective response in the actuality of singularly compelling events. (Smith, 1970:560)

All of which is to say that it is possible to locate the signifying role of conscious affect in the way things work, without taking affect to be a signifier in the sense of either an image [idea] or a chain of thought. For the universal law of the pleasure principle, Lacan has substituted the laws of language. In so doing he may have sacrificed some sense of the dynamic embodied in the pleasure principle, but that dynamic is maintained in the concepts of drive, demand, and desire that he retained. One advantage is the specification of the linguistic medium of high-level pleasure principle operation. Another advantage, notwithstanding Lacan's varied usage of "the Other," is that "the laws of language" is a concept more likely to be read as a statement of how things work than as an agency that governs.

Whatever happens in the process of disavowing or assuming, disowning or owning one's subjecthood, is constrained by the pleasure principle, constrained by the laws of language. The drives and the dynamically repressed strive for conscious realization. The pleasure principle, the laws of language, describe the ways in which that striving is or is not achieved.

TRANSFERENCE, TREATMENT, AND CURE

How might all this apply to the transference, the treatment, and the cure? Since analysis is not the only means of assuming one's subjecthood, I would like briefly to approach the issues of transference, treatment, and cure and the implicit role

of affect in them in the context of the disowning and owning
of everyday life as enacted in defensive and nondefensive repetition and ritual. Ritual, in common parlance, often implies an
unthinking, unfeeling, defensively repetitive performance. Let
us approach ritual from a different angle and from the context
of Lacan's thought.

To begin, let us set aside the usual reading, in which the central thesis of Lacan's thought is taken to be that the unconscious is
structured like a language. That thesis, central enough to be sure,
is nevertheless, like the pleasure principle, an account of how
things work rather than what makes them work. I suggest that the
central thesis in Lacan, derived more from Heidegger than from
Hegel, Saussure, or Lévi-Strauss, is that by virtue of language the
subject comes into being with a concern for that being, in accord
with which he defines the great O of his schema L (1977a:193)
as "the locus from which the question of [the subject's] existence
may be presented to him" (194).

The loss and consequent wanting in the original achievement
of separateness from the mother is the template for all subsequent loss and wanting. But this should not be taken to mean
that all desire is nothing but desire for reunion with the lost early
mother. That loss structures, sustains, colors, and echoes through
desire and the objects of desire forever, but desire is not indestructible because it has some specific object that is impossible or
because the *objet a* is ultimately nothing. Desire is indestructible,
metonymical, because its object is not that which would provide
for the satisfaction of any particular wish or demand pertaining
to needs of the desiring subject. Desire, in Lacan's view—and,
according to him, Spinoza's—"the essence of man" (1978a:107,
275), is indestructible because concern for one's being and being
with others is indestructible. Desire is futural. It reaches beyond
the satisfaction of any need or wish.

I have maintained that the concept of desire trenches upon
Freud's concept of drive, for example, "the object of desire is the
cause of the desire, and this object that is the cause of desire is

the object of the drive" (Lacan, 1978a:243). Similarly, to say that the *objet a* is the final cause of desire borders on Rapaport's emphasis that the object is a defining characteristic of the drive, with drive, of course, taken as being close to but on the psychological side of the mind-body border.

In the primal, originary loss—the turn from psychological disequilibrium as proximal source of the drive to an image of the absent object—it is the *lost* object that is constituted for a *lost* subject. Similarly, at the later stage of being born into language, "It is not from a simple opposition of the *fort* and the *da* that [the *fort-da* game] derives the inaugural force that its repetitive essence explains. To say that it is simply a question for the subject of instituting himself in a function of mastery is idiotic. In the two phonemes are embodied the very mechanisms of alienation—which are expressed, paradoxical as it may seem, at the level of the *fort*" (Lacan, 1978a:239).

It is at the point of lack and alienation that the subject can eventually come to recognize himself or herself as a subject of language. But even in the initial step, constituted by virtue of its own imaging and thus by virtue of language in the broad sense, the lost (pre)subject refinds the lost (pre)object, also initially constituted by the (pre)subject's imaging, and not the mother in her unknowable, unassimilable thingliness. Furthermore, by reason of their being linguistically constituted, the lost mother refound is never quite the same, nor is the subject who finds her. We could say there is a good enough degree of sameness for the establishment of some nondefensive constancy of both object and subject. There is also, of course, a necessary defensive holding pattern in the form of excessive claims of unity that rely on repression and disavowal of difference—difference between the refound mother and her prior appearances, difference between the subject and itself, and, for a time, difference even between the (pre)subject and the (pre)object. The way out of such a defensive trap is provided for by both the nondefensive sameness and the nonperemptory moments when difference, rather than being a threat that calls for repression or disavowal, evokes interest and attention.

Lacan wrote: "The reciprocity between the subject and the *objet a* is . . . total" (1975:114). The object is a defining characteristic of the drive. Being-with is a defining characteristic of being. I take the *objet a* to be a statement of these defining characteristics. The *objet a*, rather than referring to any object, refers to the linguistically constituted otherness/lostness of any object and thereby to a central lack in the subject. Any object or any separable aspect of the subject that comes to symbolize this central lack is in the place of the *objet a* and can function as the *objet a* (1978a:77, 103–04).

Just as the image of fulfillment originally represents the drive and thus lack, that which functions as the *objet a* symbolizes lack by an illusory promise to fill "the gap constituted by the inaugural division of the subject" (Lacan, 1978a:270).

But it never does. As promise of fulfillment forever deferred, it points toward a central lack forever present, and it is at that "point of lack that the subject has to recognize himself" (p. 270). It is thus "through the function of *objet a* [that] the subject separates himself off" (p. 258).

The *objet a* is the other (*l'autre*) of desire. It is the other and the cause of desire as desire is differentiated from wish/demand in the interplay and repetitions of difference through which a linguistically constituted subject and the otherness of the other comes to be.

Anything anyone does, thinks, or feels is a manifestation of concern for one's being and being-with. Desire at one moment, anxiety at another, arise from a want of being and a want of the other. I have suggested above, by inference from later modes of disavowal, that when the subject encounters the first signifier of its separate subjecthood, that signifier—as harbinger of the loss, lack, limit, and death that subjecthood entails—is repressed. It is turned from as a danger, but as a central, special danger that calls out not only to be faced but also—enigmatically, uncannily—to be assumed. Everything in life then becomes repetition of this central, founding encounter. Every move is, in one dimension, the repetition of either a turn toward or a turn away from this inaugural event, an event seen by Lacan as the "irreducible," "*non-sensical,*" "originally repressed signifier" that he discussed in terms of "the logical necessity of that moment in which the subject as X can be constituted only from the *Urverdrängung,* from the necessary fall of this first signifier" (1978a:251).

The motive to distance or destroy one's subjecthood and the want of being that is the mark of that subjecthood is realized as defensive repetition and the repetition compulsion. It is the central dynamic of the negative therapeutic reaction and suicide. The motive to turn toward and own one's subjecthood is realized as nondefensive repetition, what the pseudonymous (prereligious) Kierkegaard (1941:8, 33, 90) called "repetition . . . forward." If the motive to turn toward and assume one's subjecthood dominates, the (always asymptotic) approach to that accomplishment can be realized in ritual that is, at some level, both celebratory and hallowed. To the extent of that accomplishment, then, not just those shared, publicly sanctioned, sacred or secular occasions of ritual participation but all of life is embued with a dimension of ritual repetition as gratitude and celebration.

Working through is the working through of all the characteristic turnings of the analysand as these are recapitulated in the transference, without, ideally, a word ever being said about the assumption of one's subjecthood. To give direct utterance to this core concern would be wild analysis, an effort to sidestep the actual work and to jump, in alliance with the defensive wish of the analysand, to an imaginary wholeness. Instead, the analyst, able and willing to let the results of the work come in their own time and way and in terms of the analysand's specific signifiers, remains mute about the core issue while doing the daily work of bringing some small light to bear on the repressed dangers and the denied desires implicit in the equivocations of the day.

The fruit of that work does not always or even typically

announce itself in dramatic fashion. One could even wonder whether its so appearing might be, in part, a function of the desire of the analyst for such vivid acknowledgment of the cure. However, for whatever reasons, it does at times so appear, and those appearances may shed light on what has occurred behind the scene in other cures. At some level, whether dramatically revealed or not, the fruit of analytic work, finally, is that the analysand comes face to face with . . . what? With nothingness? With loss, lack, and limit? With the originally repressed signifier of one's subjecthood? With "Now that I am nothing . . . I am made to be a man?"*

I have insisted that no affective response exists independently of *some* signifier of which it is the context. This, however, does not rule out the existence of compelling moments that can only be considered moments of insight in which extremes of affective response seem virtually empty of conscious signifiers. Such a moment, whether in dread, awe, gratitude (though not merely gratitude toward the analyst), or unnameable affect, might be what I have called the affective equivalent of facing the originally repressed signifier of one's subjecthood.

*From Lacan's reading of *Oedipus at Colonus* (*Séminaire* II, 1978, as cited in Felman, 1987:132).

CHAPTER SIX

THE FATHER OF INDIVIDUAL PREHISTORY AND THE IDEALS OF THE ANALYST

My purpose here is to consider the place of defensive and nondefensive identification in development as a basis for understanding modes of allegiance among psychoanalysts to particular psychoanalytic heroes or ideas. How is it that one's heroes become established, and how do those heroes and the set of ideas associated with them sustain one's daily work? Finally, I shall attempt to conceptualize defensive and nondefensive modes of allegiance in terms of allegiance that prohibits going beyond a precursor and allegiance that precisely fosters such innovation and growth. In the effort to elucidate nondefensive orthodoxy, it might be mentioned that the "ortho" of orthodox, from the Greek *ortho* (straight), had its Indo-European base in *werdh*—to grow, to climb, and thus to achieve height.

My guiding hunch is this: heroes and heroines exemplify the validity of an early trust established by virtue of that which Freud named the father of individual prehistory (*Standard Edition*, 19:31). As I mentioned in chapter 3, I take this trust to be in a different register from that which the infant develops in the dual relationship with the mother. Nondefensively established heroes and heroines, I will argue, do not become the *objects* of the trust.

They are instead taken as models exemplifying the validity of trust in one's self and the world and the courage that such trust can generate.

THIRD TERMS AND THE PATERNAL FUNCTION

We have seen that Lacan took the "name of the father" (from the Judeo-Christian heritage via Freud's *Totem and Taboo*; see Lacan, 1977a:199, 1978a:281–82) as metaphor for the paternal function. The symbolic paternal function in the oedipal crisis is the finally effective third term that mediates symbolic castration, the law against incest, the release from the dual mode of relating, and thus accession to the symbolic order as embodied in a particular culture. The name of the father in Shoshana Felman's phrasing stands for "the first authoritative 'no,' the first social imperative of renunciation, inaugurating . . . both the necessity of repression and the process of symbolic substitution of objects of desire, which Lacan calls 'the Symbolic'" (1987:104).

But, in general, a third term can be taken as any factor that unsettles the oneness and self-sameness presumably experienced in moments of symbiotic tranquility. Any primarily given or secondarily established trait, function, or structure that serves to maintain nondefensive differentiation is a third term. By nondefensive differentiation I mean differentiation in which loss, lack, and limit are owned. To speak of "the finally effective third term" points to a whole series of third terms that have from the beginning initiated differentiation or difference as opposed to self-sameness or identificatory sameness with the dual or imaginary object.

The first third term is delay itself, the inevitable delay in the satisfaction of need that evokes imaging and affect. The infant's self-sameness in physiological equilibrium is thrown out of kilter, and on the basis of that and the primarily given capacities for perception, imaging, affect, memory, and anticipation, imagery achieves semiotic status. Though not yet known to the infant, the image and affect are of and for the mother and represent the need. The move, then, from the identity of perception to the identity of thought—coming to know the difference between an image and a percept—is a step in differentiation initiated by the third term of delay and maintained by the preconscious organization implied by the identity of thought.

Differentiation first of all prepares the way for a dual relationship. It is first self-sameness that is disturbed, divided, ruptured; this leads to a progressive organization in primary process thinking that establishes the capacity for dual, identificatory relatedness with the mother. The relatedness is of a self-object nature, to be sure, but already the subject is divided, not identical with itself, and the object is, in some measure, already other.

I take Freud's concept of the father of individual prehistory and Lacan's concept of the paternal function as referring to all third terms that initiate and sustain early differentiation. These factors point the child toward a world beyond the dual, identificatory, narcissistic, imaginary mode of relating to the mother. It is in this sense that the father of individual prehistory is not an object and thus not an object for identification.

The factors that initiate and sustain nondefensive differentiation evoke imagery, the primitive organization of imagery, and, eventually, the preconscious organization—the unity that completes the formative steps that release the innate human capacity for speech. This is to say that the paternal function has its effects by virtue of language in the broad sense of a system that orders not only speech but also primitive imaging.

WHERE ID WAS THERE EGO SHALL BE

I subscribe to Harold Bloom's view of development as a series of catastrophes (Smith, 1980b:ix–xiii; Bloom, 1980:20–21). Each step in the disturbance of a given or achieved unity is an experience of loss, thrownness, nothingness, anxiety, castration, and death. To develop is to confront one danger situation after another—danger situations from which one tends to turn away. But to compound the complexity, whatever is turned away from is marked as a danger to be faced or a loss to be mourned. We are self-divided from that which we are called upon to mourn or to face or to be.

That which is repressed is indestructible, not only because wishes neither satisfied nor renounced endure, and not only because the repressed becomes associated with the drives that are always pressing for conscious realization and enactment. Also accounting for the indestructibility of the repressed are the desire arising from insurmountable want of being—desire as manifestation of concern for one's being—and the institution of subordinate centers of ego disequilibrium by each act of repression. The subordinate centers also press for conscious realization and enactment. Whether heeded or not, one is called upon at every moment to turn and face that from which one flees. In Freud's phrasing, "where id was there ego shall be" (*Standard Edition*, 22:80).

Notwithstanding the repetition of danger and loss and even the ongoing catastrophe of being self-divided, one survives, and that is rightly attributed to the mother's care and love. What I am here calling trust associated with the father of individual prehistory arises, I think, from affectively more neutral sources than the trust, love, and identification with the early mother. It is, I would suggest, derived from the gradual realization that no matter how large the catastrophes, no matter how little one comprehends, whatever goes on is ordered. That is to say it is structured and systematic and has meaning prior to one's recognition of that structure, systematicity, or meaning. The senseless, fragmentary, original image—it comes to be known—is of the mother. Not only that, the image and the metonymically elaborated and metaphorically founded and organized system of substitute images open up a world, a world in which one can, eventually, come to be. The notion of a father of individual prehistory is retrospectively attributed not only to the primitive third terms that disrupt unity but also to the linguistically constituted and ordered world that comes to be established in the resolution of such disruptions. The father of individual prehistory is, in this sense, the mythical father of that world.

The world is just the way the system works. The system is brought into play by the situation of need, delay, and the infant's innate capacities. The first instance in which the dynamic of the system is evoked is also the first step in the organization of the self and the basis for an initial glimpse of a world in which mother and infant can come to have their separate being. However, throughout development, unconscious knowledge of the system that structures one's existence always exceeds that of conscious knowledge.

Freud's concept for conveying the systematicity of these organizing steps was that of the pleasure principle in its most general sense. Lacan sought to convey systematicity by showing that the unconscious is structured like a language—subject, that is, just like conscious processes though under different conditions, to the rule-orderedness or lawlike effects of language as a system. An example of the way Lacan took to concretize that meaning and also to remind us that it was already there in the Freudian text was the emphasis he gave to those passages where Freud spoke of perceptual traces as being constituted in simultaneity "by virtue," as Lacan put it, "of a very defined structure of constituent diachrony." Lacan asked, "What is this [simultaneity] . . . , if not signifying synchrony?" (1978a:46).

I again invoke these instances of Freudian and Lacanian thought to illustrate developmental factors that instigate and mediate differentiation prior to the oedipal era. My argument is that these factors, retrospectively, come to be symbolized by some notion of a father of individual prehistory. They are the differentiating power of what comes to be seen as the paternal function in any person's prehistory. This is to say that the paternal function of the oedipal father as the finally effective third term intervening in the mother-child duality becomes associated after the fact with all the preoedipal factors that also so intervened. The most primitive of these, such as early delay, were not points of identification. The early differentiating factors are boundary-setting phenomena. Subsequently, aspects of relationships with objects can be either defensively or nondefensively internalized because internality and externality have been constituted.

SUBJECTHOOD AND WORLDHOOD

Disturbances in early life tend to be personified. One can infer from depressive modes of being that they can be experienced as punishments implying guilt (Smith, 1986b). From heroic modes of being it can be inferred that disturbances can also come to be experienced as a way of being called or awakened to the world, to one's own subjecthood, and to one's ideal way of being in the world.

The "father" of personal prehistory, Freud noted, is a function of both parents.* The mother is the first to be in the place of the Other. It is she who initially mediates lack, limit, finitude, language, and the world. Identification with the "father" of individual prehistory begins as identification with signifiers of the mother's nonnarcissistic way of being in the world. But the father, as the main other of the mother/infant unity, comes to be the symbol of all the factors challenging symbiotic unity and defensive denial of separateness and limit in the preoedipal dual relationship with the mother.

The father as symbol of, in Felman's words, the first authoritative no, the father feared, the father as giver of the law, is the forerunner of the superego arising in the wake of the oedipal crisis. But the father of individual prehistory, the forerunner of the ego ideal, antedates either the feared or beloved father. He

*Freud wrote, "Perhaps it would be safer to say 'with the parents' . . . [but] in order to simplify my presentation I shall discuss only identification with the father" (*Standard Edition*, 19:31n; cf. 18:105–07).

is there, brought into view by the mother's way of being in a world and by her wish for her child to enter that world. It is the father as the first and foremost other who is the representative and mediator of that world and that future.*

By being other to the symbiotic pair, the early father (or the father—a father [Lacan, 1977a:217]—as mediated to the child from early childhood by the mother) is a figure, a model, representing the achievement of separate being in a world toward which the child, boy or girl, can move. Because he is not the object of peremptory need, his specific traits and his otherness can be nonperemptorily appraised and adopted as model. He comes to represent, as the symbolic father, all factors promoting and sustaining differentiation. The child's unconscious endopsychic perception of a sustaining order/regulation/systematization is unconsciously attributed to the father, who sustains the mother even in his absence. The identification or modeling that occurs is unconscious. From the point of view of conscious experience, the child finds himself or herself being in a way that can be recognized as like the parent. It is an affirming recognition.

Of course, virtually everything said here about the father is equally true of the mother. In nonperemptory moments, she also is other and thus the first to be in the place of the Other. However, the evolution in the mind of the child of the symbolic mother is influenced by the memory of her as object of peremptory need.

The symbolic father, derived ultimately from both the father of individual prehistory and the oedipal father/precursor of the superego, represents the law, the symbolic order, the future, the world, and a nonnarcissistic mode of being in the world that the mother initially mediated.

*This implies neither maternality as masochism (see the chapter following) nor, even though a hardship for the mother and child, an actual father who is physically on the scene. The essential is a mother not driven to see herself as author of her own being and the child as only an extension of her being.

The symbolic mother represents source in oneness from which one comes and to which, in both desire and death, one returns. The introduction of limit comes to be associated with the paternal function, but lack and limit, the want of being that is the source of desire, are originally encountered in relation to the mother as absent object. Good-enough mothering is to return to the child sufficiently to instill trust, but, even more crucially, to return in such a way as to foster and sustain the child's eventual acknowledgment of an internally inscribed, insurmountable loss, dividedness, and wanting. Such acknowledgment occurs where the mother instills trust in herself in the process of mediating a world also worthy of trust.

The symbolized mother is the absent mother. The world that opens up with the image, the signifier, the chain of signifiers, begins as an effort to fill in a lack. But by virtue of language and the paternal function, this effort culminates in a world in which the inherency of lack is revealed and can be acknowledged and owned. The initial tendency to internalize aspects of the relationship with the mother as a denial of lack models the dual mode of relating with the preoedipal mother and all subsequent defensive identification.

The capacity to turn and face danger, lack, loss, and limit depends on subjection to the name of the father, but it is a kind of subjection that is also a nondefensive identification with the name of the father as mediated by both the mother and the father. "Objectless" identification with the father of individual prehistory is a first step toward recognition and acknowledgment of a subjecthood that is structured, recognized, and identified by both parents in the place of the Other—both parents as mediators of the symbolic order. Symbolic identification, as I understand it, has nothing to do with the internalization of any particular idiosyncratic trait. It is instead the recognition that one is like one's parents in the same sense that one is like every other human. One shares with them the lot of what it is to be a human being. This comes to pass in the oedipal era as a finally effective identification for both the boy and the girl, an identification that signifies symbolic castration achieved. It is the recapitulation of the early identification with the name of the father, an indwelling of recognition in the sense of both recognizing and being recognized.

This dimension of "identification" in the resolution of the oedipal crisis is, I believe, essential and essentially the same for both boy and girl. Like a second work of grace, it is both the recapitulation of and the product of the nonperemptory and thus nonnarcissistic (that is, not motivated by the necessity of denying separateness) "identification" with the father of individual prehistory in earliest childhood. If that early identification is not really identification at all but transference, as Kristeva maintains (1987a:25, 1987b:27), its oedipal recapitulation will be something like the resolution of the transference. We can again recall Freud's words: "whatever the character's later capacity for resisting the influences of abandoned object-cathexis may turn out to be, the effects of the first identifications made in earliest childhood will be general and lasting" (*Standard Edition*, 18:105).

To summarize my own view, to the extent that identification with the father of individual prehistory *is* an identification *or* transference, it is imaginary—identification with or transference to an image of the father. To the extent that it is recognition of sustaining order/regulation/systematization, it is a recognition and a being recognized by the symbolic father, the symbolic order.

If everything I have here listed does tend to become attributed to some sense of a father of individual prehistory, then, if not a myth itself, it is the stuff of which myths are made. I have attempted to show reasons for believing it to be the latter and not the former, meaning that those nonperemptory interactions that constitute what Freud called an identification with the father of individual prehistory actually do occur. When Lacan spoke of this first form of identification as "a mythical stage, certainly," he indicated a disbelief that such early "identification" as founding recognition could occur. For the father of individual prehistory

he substituted the *einziger Zug*, the single stroke, the first signifier, the passage into language, which he placed in the field of
desire "at a level in which there is a relation of the subject to the
Other" (1978a:256).

This entire book could be taken as an effort to show that these
apparently competing interpretations are compatible. Speech announces separateness, otherness, which the father had represented all along. Language in the broad sense, reaching back to
the first traces and images, is both the sign of and the means of
achieving separateness. The lawlike effects of language become
retrospectively identified with the father of individual prehistory,
who was, already then, the father of one's future, the father of
the word, *the* word.

Kristeva wrote of "the drive/body splitting, which initiates the
setting up of psychic space" (1987b:315). I have located this splitting (primal repression) at the very first turn from bodily need,
as represented in psychic disequilibrium, toward an affect-laden
image of the object. This move is regulated, in my view, *by* the
pleasure principle, rather than being an overcoming by the drive
of the pleasure principle seen as only a homeostatic principle on
the real or "body" side of the mind/body border. Regulation,
ordering, systematization, is already there in the initial setting up
of psychic space.

I cite again a passage from Lacan, but this time without
apology for perhaps bending his meaning toward mine: "The
Other is already there in the very opening, however evanescent,
of the unconscious" (*Séminaire* XI, 1973, as cited by Felman,
1987:22).

PHALLOCENTRISM, THE IDEAL EGO, AND THE EGO IDEAL

Through symbolic castration the relinquishment of
defensive phallocentrism is achieved. Defensive or imaginary
castration is suffered or feared. Symbolic castration is achieved

through owning the inherency of dividedness, lack, and limit. In defensive phallocentrism lack and limit are seen as contingent. Lack of the phallus is contingent. The mother or the girl may have been castrated or perhaps have a hidden phallus. The imaginary phallus that one has lost or may lose or that is hidden serves, then, to deny the inherency of lack. Only with the relinquishment of defensive phallocentrism can the phallus nondefensively symbolize difference, desire, the paternal function, the third term between mother and child, procreative reunion, life, love, and, thereby, the copula of metaphorization. It is then that the phallus can symbolize symbolization itself.* Women, because they begin with imaginary lack, with imaginary castration rather than the fear of it, are less defended and thus have a better chance of relinquishing defensive phallocentrism. I take that to be a core element of womanly wisdom (Smith, 1980a).

When Freud wrote that identification with the father of individual prehistory was direct and immediate[†] he was, I take it, referring to a relatively conflict-free dimension of achieving subjecthood in a world—of being like the father and of relating to the father as first other—that the boy or girl takes into the oedipal encounter with the father as object. The product of that "objectless" identification with the "father" is the established ego ideal.

What the child learns from the mother is that some disturbances, even though they enter the scene as dangers, institute the development of subjecthood and being in a world. This learning is modeled on the child's experience, when need is not at a peremptory level, of "disturbances" that do not signal danger but instead evoke the child's attention, interest, and play. I have

---

*I have been unable to find the advantage of giving the organ one name (the penis) and reserving another (the phallus) for that of which it can be the symbol. So far as I am concerned a rose is a rose and a phallus is a penis. As Gallop (1981) puts it, "same difference."

†See Kristeva, "An 'Immediate' and Objectless Identification" (1987b:26).

suggested that the signifiers intimating one's own separate sub-jecthood probably first arise in such nonperemptory moments. It is likely, that is, that one plays one's way into awareness of separateness as a danger—a danger in a wholly different register from both the danger of physical neediness in the absence of the mother and the danger of the instinctual drives.

No doubt the perception of the danger of separate subject-hood and the ways of defending against it are influenced by the mother's basic way of being in the world. However, as Kier-kegaard wrote, "that which is genuinely human no generation learns from the foregoing" (1954:130). Some things cannot be taught; some things each individual has to learn on his or her own. Separate subjecthood, I assume, presents itself first of all as a significant danger, no matter how ideal the mothering, and no matter the innate sensitivity to separateness with which the infant is born—the latter surely one factor in schizophrenic foreclosure of the name of the father.

The danger of separate subjecthood is uncanny because it comes also as a reminder of a dividedness within; it is a danger not external to the core of one's being, as are dangers such as hunger, thirst, cold, or physical pain. It is a danger that one is called upon not just to face but to assume. And unlike the drives that are also of the core of one's being, it is not a danger for which the object can provide relief.

HEROINES, HEROES, NEW PATIENTS, AND ALLEGIANCE TO ONE PSYCHOANALYTIC THEORY OR ANOTHER

Primitive, defensive, peremptory identifications tend to be indiscriminately total internalizations of the relationship with the object (Smith, 1971). To so identify with the mother is a defense against the dawning realization of one's separateness from her and of one's inner dividedness. Imaginary identification with the object in this total way serves to perpetuate original sym-biosis or the dual narcissistic attachment of the preoedipal era.

In more advanced, nonperemptory, nondefensive identifications, specific aspects of the relationship with the object are internalized. But core identifications that foster and reflect both subjecthood and worldhood I am here describing as identification with the father of individual prehistory. To some extent, as has been mentioned, that means identification with the mother's nonnarcissistic stance. But to some extent it is simply recognizing that the mother's way of being in a world beyond that of only herself and her child matches and affirms incipient steps in that direction already undertaken by the child on its own. "Objectless identification" I take as referring to this element of affirming recognition.

Resolution of the oedipal crisis allows for assumption of one's gender and subjecthood and obviates the necessity of subsequent defensive identification. But resolution is always relative, and one is forever encountering new third terms and forever repeating resolution. Resolution of the oedipal crisis doesn't mean not having to face new third terms; it means being able to negotiate in relatively nondefensive fashion the reworking of repetitions of the original crisis.

If the oedipal crisis has been resolved so that subsequent similar crises can be nondefensively faced, the choice of one's heroines or heroes is celebratory. They represent the ideals of courage and wisdom toward which one strives as a separate subject. To the extent that oedipal resolution has been hampered, the need for a heroine or a hero is a bit like the need for heroin. It may, in fact, be a kind of addiction. It is also, of course, a quest for a way out of the preoedipal dual mode of relating, but it is at the same time a compulsive need to maintain the preoedipal mode of relating, with the heroine or hero now as object. The consequence is often that the heroine or hero does not prove to be a third term that effectively carries one over to the symbolic order. Instead the dual mode of relating to the mother is simply transferred to the new object. This is transference as resistance, transference that refuses a differentiating struggle with one's imaginarily constituted parent or precursor.

To the extent that this mode of transference characterizes the

analyst's allegiance to a certain psychoanalytic theory, it is defensive orthodoxy. I have emphasized Freud's notion of identification with the father of individual prehistory as trust in one's
own courage and power to face danger, third terms, and the
new in ways that allow for change and growth. I take this to be
the paradigm for nondefensive identification and nondefensive
orthodoxy.

I write here, of course, in terms of polar extremes. I assume
that we all live out our lives and our professional lives in some
degree of both defensive and nondefensive allegiance to certain
individuals and groups and ideas associated with them. In terms
of one's relationship with precursors and those persons and ideas
associated with them, a new patient enters the scene as a third
term. In the conflict of defensive and nondefensive orthodoxies,
the patient presents on the one hand the threat of unsettling
one's accustomed mode of thinking and on the other the opportunity to learn something new, to engage in an adventure of insight that will depart in some way from previously held beliefs.
Kristeva wrote: "In transference the analyst risks the dissolution
of his own knowledge, that is, of what the patient presumes his
knowledge to be and of the knowledge that he has brought to
bear in other cases. Each analysis modifies—or should modify—
at least some of the beliefs about psychodynamics that I held before hearing what the analysand had to say" (1987a:51). Lacan,
similarly, wrote of the analyst's "ignorance of each subject who
comes to him for analysis, of an ever renewed ignorance that
prevents anyone becoming a 'case'" (1977a:322).

The threat of change in one's accustomed ways of thinking,
which often accompanies the entrance of a new analysand on the
scene, could strike one as not a crucial matter—a matter only
of alteration of theory. To the contrary, my purpose in associ-
ating nondefensive orthodoxy with the nondefensive identification with the father of individual prehistory has been to address
the core significance of precursors and one's allegiance to and
struggle with them, which is forever renewed in one's life and

work. The texts of one's precursors are constantly being challenged and altered, knowingly or unknowingly, in the light of
one's daily work. That means that core aspects of one's subjecthood and way of being in the world are being challenged and
altered as one approaches core issues of the patient in analytic
work. For this reason, whether one's allegiance to precursors is
dominantly defensive or nondefensive, a new analysand is at least
as apt to evoke sobriety as joyful anticipation of new adventure.

CHAPTER SEVEN

EVENING THE SCORE

For purposes of tracing some implications of the transition from symbiosis to the symbolic order, it may be useful to draw a distinction between the symbiotic mother and the symbolic mother. The symbiotic mother is the mother of the undifferentiated stage, the mother of the preverbal era who is not yet other. But, at the risk of overschematization, let us stretch the ordinary meaning of symbiosis so that the symbiotic mother refers to all stages of differentiation prior to the oedipal era. The symbiotic mother would then be the mother first imaged as the object of wish-fulfillment; the mother as self-object in Kohutian terms; the imaginary mother, in the language of Lacan, who mirrors an image of unity to the infant; and, even, the mother of the dual relationship from the time the advent of speech announces her as other until her fundamental relinquishment in the symbolic castration achieved during the oedipal crisis.

The symbolic mother is not only the mother that comes to be known as other by virtue of language and the oedipal crisis; she is also, as Lacan phrased it, the mother in the place of the Other. This is to say that the symbolic mother is the mother who has all along introduced language and mediated being in the place of the Other to the father. It is she whose nonnarcissistic mode of being in the world points the child toward the father and a future apart from herself. It is this dimension of both the mother and the father with which the child identifies in what Freud called "identification with the father . . . [of] personal prehistory" (*Standard Edition*, 19:31).

To the extent that the mother is defensively narcissistic, to the extent, that is, that she sees the child as an extension of herself, as her phallus, she is the symbiotic mother resisting the child's transition to the symbolic order. To the extent that the child's desire, also in narcissistic defensiveness, is the desire of the mother, to the extent that the child's wish is to be the phallus of the mother, the mother thus structured is the mother of symbiosis.

In sum, the symbiotic mother is the mother of merger, the symbolic mother the mother of separateness as here elaborated. The motive to return to the mother can be primarily to return to the symbiotic mother or primarily to find or refind the symbolic mother. The latter would not be just a regression to the past but a refinding of the first mediator of one's future and of the symbolic order. The symbolic mother, then, refers not only to the mother as known by virtue of having entered the symbolic order, but also to that which the mother thus known can symbolize—to the maternal as symbol.

With this as introduction, I here offer a dual commentary with Julia Kristeva's complex response to Lacanian (and Freudian) phallocentrism as text. The style follows that employed by Kristeva in "Stabat Mater" (1986:160–86; also in Kristeva, 1987b:234–63), which Toril Moi describes as "deliberate typographical fragmentation of the page" (in Kristeva, 1986:160).

In "The 'Chora,' Receptacle of Narcissism," a section of *Powers of Horror* (1982), Kristeva carries what is for her the always recurring story of primal repression to the scene of incest and its taboo. "Curious primacy, where what is repressed cannot be held down, and where what represses always already borrows its strength and authority from what is apparently very secondary: language. Let us therefore not speak of primacy but of the instability of the symbolic function in its most significant aspect—the prohibition placed on the maternal body. . . . Here [in the place of what is repressed] drives hold sway and constitute a strange space that I shall name, after Plato (Timeus, 48–53) a *chora*, a receptacle" (pp. 13–14).

There is a question here of what is to be given the primacy of being primal—the decentering chora, that "strange space" where "the drives hold sway," or the (phallic and phallo-centering) image, sign, or symbolic function. What is more primal—that which is repressed or that which re-presses? At a glance, one might think that that which is to be repressed has priority. The trouble is that what is to be repressed is not constituted as such until a "repressing" image, sign, or structure comes into play. At the most primi-tive level, the "repressed" or "abject" can only be taken as that which is turned away from and the "repressing" as the

In the beginning according to Kristeva, was the Word ——— (within the chora). The latter, cradle of the drives and of the images and affects representing but also pitted against the drives, "a strange space that I shall name . . . a *chora*, a receptacle."

In the beginning was the Chora ——— (within which came to pass the word).

Does not every mother believe her male child to be a God and herself to be the proud mother, wife, and daughter of this God of her own flesh, her own making, and thus the only being prop-erly to be honored as son, father, husband, God? Could any actual, human husband match this, reserved-only-for-the-son, investment? Are not the seeds of all phallocen-trism here? Does not all male narcissism have its source in maternal narcissism?

And what happens when a second son is born? Was this the source of Cain's agitation? Could the endeavor of the brothers really have been toward the favor of a Father, let alone a father?

How could a son work through and out of this trap? Is there not need of a name of the father beyond merely that of, say, Joseph, or would that be only to become more enmeshed?

Simone de Beauvoir had it wrong, indeed, to see in the nativity of Piero della Francesca a feminine defeat because the mother kneeled before her barely born son (Kristeva, 1986:171). Think of it from the son's point of view. I mean the kid was too young to know, but who could want to be a God knowing that the bowed head of one's mother "is accompanied by the immeasurable pride of the one who knows she is also his wife and daughter. She knows *she* [my italics] is destined to that eternity (of the spirit or of the species), of which every mother is unconsciously aware, and with regard to which maternal turning itself, together with that to which the turning is directed. This is what it means to say that the drives are not autochthonous givens. They are constituted and shaped in early experience. Through the mother's mediation, what is repressed and that which represses constitute each other.

At first, they are not differentiated. There is an analogy—at some level an identity—here between the most primitive and that most advanced "specially perfect functioning" dear to the heart of Freud, where id, ego, and superego all work together as one. Early imaging can still be seen as a splitting in that there is a turning away from devotion or even sacrifice is but an insignificant price to pay. A price that is borne all the more easily since, contrasted with the love that binds a mother to her son, all other 'human relationships' burst like blatant shams" (p. 172).

But what could be more a sham than this? It's a trap. The mother, within the enclosure of her own narcissism extended to include the son, may regard it as an insignificant price to pay, but it is one hell of a price she is extracting from the son.

The crucial questions pertaining to nondefensive and defensive phallocentrism are these: *Is*, in fact, the enthronement of the son as God merely an extension of maternal narcissism, or did a male God arise as a step in woman's renunciation of her own divinity, the veneration of Mary being projection as a compromise between retention and renunciation? Or did a male God arise from sons (with the help of their fathers) as a way out of, or at least a mode of resisting, the narcissistic maternal enclosure that robs them of their humanity?

something, but there is nothing *conflictual* about *primal* repression so long as that expression is reserved for only that never-to-be-witnessed-or-known first turning. There, it can only be presumed, the drive drives toward the image of the object. In so doing, the drive drives toward the object, we say, even though there is as yet no drive, no desire, no wish, no object, differentiated from each other. The image of the object represents the drive. The image *is,* at once, drive, desire, wish, object.

It is through the mother's mediation that the difference between the identity of perception and the identity of thought, the difference be-

Actually, it can go either way and is always, to some extent, a mix. However, it is both more fun and truer to the subjective extremes to pursue, for a while, each possibility as though it and it alone were preordained.

Could the veneration of Mary and motherhood perhaps be, after all, a vain effort of revenge visited by sons (and the fathers of the church) against mothers in which the mother is deprived of sex, death, and therefore life, in a way that matches the threat to the son enthroned by her as God? Could not one source of the motive to incest be an effort to break out of the divine enclosure by touching the mother at the level of her own and the son's own humanity?

It is uncertain. However, one thing is clear. Whether a male God derives from mothers, by renunciation *or* extension of maternal narcissism, or from sons (and fathers) as resistance to the maternal enclosure, or both, to the extent that He still is, He is definitively male. Can anyone believe that merely rewriting the Bible to make Him neuter, or either male

tween the image of the object and the object itself, is established. This is Freud's first phrasing of the turn from primary process to secondary process, or, rather, his phrasing of the first phase of that turning. It is a second level of splitting, beyond that of the primal turning away from unmet need as danger. The image is reduced to a "mere" image and the object to a "mere" object. But *prior* to the differentiation of the identity of perception and the identity of thought, the image has a fullness that, in language, only the poetic word recaptures.

In the beginning was ———
I have not the slightest idea. A chicken *and* an egg? Drive

or female, or both male and female, could render Him otherwise? It was bad enough to revise at all the version bestowing Grace, Mercy, and Peace, and done, *by the Grace of God, for "The Most High and Mighty Prince James, King of Great Britain, France, and Ireland, Defender of the Faith, Etc.,"* whatever *Etc.* might have meant. Those earlier revisions, though, like most committee decisions, were merely wrong. But to fool around with the sex of God is crazy. What next? Will we have, as in someone's cartoon, a touch-up of the Sistine ceiling—a beardless God with an even wider ass touching the outstretched finger of a curvaceous Eve?

Come to think of it . . . *and* image? An undifferentiated id/ego? Drive *and* reality-determined syncretic perception?

Perhaps, though nothing to crow about, it would be safe to say that in the beginning, well, shortly after the beginning, was the drive *and* reality determined, drive *and* reality representing, affect-laden syncretic image, based on the memory of a prior experience of satisfaction. That we take as the beginning, at least so far as thinking (at this level, ideation, that is, thinking in images) is concerned.

The memory of a prior experience of satisfaction is a memory of the object before the object is established as object. The image thus "represents" both drive and the "not yet" object. The first image is the first "not yet" metaphor. It is not only a precursor of the word that, by a relationship of differential opposition to all other words in a language, will come to designate the object. It is also, by virtue of being the infant's "all," a precursor of the metaphorical object, the Great Other, of language as all-structuring system into which the infant will later be born.

The turn from unmet need as danger to an image of the object is the original scene of primal repression, "the very splitting that establishes the psyche and . . . bends the drive towards the symbolic of an other. Only the metaphorical dynamics (in the sense of a *heterogenous* displacement shattering the isotopy of organic needs) justifies that this other be a Great Other" (Kristeva, 1987b:31).

The writing of Kristeva's "Stabat Mater" (from the opening words of the hymn, "Stabat mater dolorosa"—"Stood the Mother, full of grief") "coincides," Toril Moi writes, "with her own experience of maternity, recorded and reflected in the personal observations which break up the main body of the text" (Kristeva, 1986:160).

A daughter is more permitted her humanity, a maternal gift and deprivation that ensures, among other things, a continuing source of both the divine and the human to come.

The chora? The daughter is the more direct recipient of the chora that everyone has or is but only mothers really know about. (In precise opposition to the defensive or nondefensive status of the phallus, so far as the chora is concerned, if you only *have* it, it's imaginary. You have to *be* it or forget it.)

The only thing that can be said with certainty about the chora is that it pulsates—at least that is the word used by those who think about what is most central as the heart of hearts. Those who asso-

It is Kristeva's explicit assumption that we live in a civilization where "the *consecrated* (religious or secular) representation of femininity is absorbed by motherhood" (p. 161). It is also her explicit assumption that this concept of motherhood, "one of the most ciate the chora more with the drives and sexuality are apt to say it throbs.

Serious thinkers remind us of the paradox that what is most central is, at once, always also most marginal. Even the ordinary person can vouch for the fact that it is never clear whether the pulsating is inside or outside. Sometimes the whole world seems to throb.

Even if others have or are a chora, the maternal chora is clearly the most dangerous. It can comfort you to death. It is the maternal chora that can drive a son crazy, partly because he doesn't know *where* it is and keeps looking in the wrong place, but mostly because he can't know *what* it is.

But it is a problem not just for sons. Out of awe of the unknown, both little boys and little girls attribute to the mother a hidden phallus as a way of covering the chora. Some analysts believe that the fearsomeness of this particular phallus arises because it *is* a phallus, and see in the head of Medusa fright multiplied because of multiple phalluses. Lacanians, on the other hand,

powerful imaginary constructs known in the history of civilizations" (p. 163), is, for both men and women, a defensive, imaginary "*fantasy* . . . of a lost territory . . . the idealization of the *relationship* that binds us to [the archaic mother] . . . an idealization of primary narcissism" (p. 161). For women in particular, it is "a way of dealing with feminine paranoia" (p. 180).

Within that perspective, Kristeva addresses two questions: "What is there, in the portrayal of the Maternal in general and particularly in its Christian, virginal, one, that as is their wont, say that the English and American analysts who think this way have it all wrong. The snakes are not frightening because they are phalluses; they are frightening because each snake is a denial of castration. It is then sort of like the club that Tolstoy and his brothers and cousins formed, in which the whole idea of the club was not to think about a white bear.

However, as is my wont as I write here at Deep Creek Lake on Mother's Day, year of our Lord, 1987, I can tell you that they are all wrong. Little boys do not attribute a phallus to the mother out of fear of castration; little girls do not attribute a hidden phallus to their mothers and themselves in order to deny castration; and mothers do not see their infants as phalluses out of a primary desire for the phallus.

The whole issue of being or not being the phallus or of having or not having a phallus is thoroughly secondary, derivative, and defensive. It makes for a strange chorography in the land of gender. A phallus, that obvious, protruding, substantial thing, is reduces social anguish and gratifies a male being; what is there that also satisfies a woman so that a commonality of the sexes is set up, beyond and in spite of their glaring incompatibility and permanent warfare?" (p. 163).

From the assumption that the concept of femininity and the maternal is defensive, it follows that any male gratification or female satisfaction, or commonality of the sexes thus set up, will also be defensive, imaginary.

Notwithstanding this explicit bias in the text toward an interpretation of the Marian ascribed, overtly or covertly, to everyone in an anxiety-ridden, defensive effort to cover the chora.

The maternal phallus is not the most frightening because it is a phallus, or because it is hidden, or because it is a denial of castration; the maternal phallus is most frightening because it covers the most awesome chora.

Everyone is implicated in phallocentrism. Phallocentrism is comforting. Deconstructing or fighting against phallocentrism is a denial that one has already secretly adopted it as a defense. There will always be more than just rumors of war between the sexes. The war is essential to preserve the myth that phallocentrism *is* the central issue that one should be called upon to uphold, feel guilty about, or undermine and fight against. That is the most effective means of denying that phallocentrism is a defense and a cover.

This is politically defensive phallocentrism, whether fought for or against. As a defense, either to uphold or to deconstruct phallocentrism is a distraction, a way of

Cult as defensive (in opposition to the marginal interpretation of motherhood), there is also at work in the text an opposite, implicit interpretation of the Marian Cult as non-defensive. "The Mother and her attributes, evoking sorrowful humanity, thus become representatives of a 'return of the repressed' in monotheism. They reestablish what is non-verbal and show up as the receptacle of a signifying disposition that is closer to so-called primary processes. Without them the complexity of the Holy Ghost would have been mutilated. On the other

defending against knowing
that the phallus and all the
fighting about it represses
the chora. Ultimately, the
warfare ensures a continuing
defensive stance in relation
to the chora. It is a mode of
the imaginary—a mode of
being rather than having or
not having the phallus. Only
he or she who can face (face?
is there another word?) the
chora can have or not have a
phallus.

hand, as they return by way
of the Virgin Mother, they
find their outlet in the arts—
painting and music—of which
the Virgin necessarily becomes both patron saint and
privileged object" (p. 174).

The implication—unnoted in "Stabat Mater"—is that if the abject, here instanced by "the Mother and her attributes," is the source of the arts, it is the source not only of wordless painting and music but also (by virtue of the departure from the every-day, commonsense or scientific use of words) of literature and religion. Painting, music, literature, and religion are sublimated signifiers of the abject as source, even though the monotheistic God be male.

The arts, literature, and religion are sublimated, enduring versions of how it is that the abject, in moments of narcissistic crisis, upholds the "I." The abject (all that is turned away from, in-cluding, with time, the primitive, pre-objectal mother originally turned toward) returns as muse. Works of art and religion enter into the cultural order, the space of the Other, upholding "I," upholding the Other, upholding "I" within the Other, humanity within the Other.

It is a curious upholding. Cultural objects uphold by virtue of being enduring reminders of source and destiny. They uphold by calling upon the I, upon humanity, to face that from which it tends to turn away.

"The function of this 'Virginal Maternal' may thus be seen

taking shape in the Western symbolic economy. Starting with the
high Christly sublimation for which it yearns . . . and extend-
ing to the extralinguistic regions of the unnameable, the Virgin
Mother occupied the tremendous territory hither and yon of the
parenthesis of language. She adds to the Christian trinity and to
the Word that delineates their coherence the heterogeneity they
salvage" (1986: 174–75).

The Word, associated with God the Father, delineates coherence within an encompassing maternal dimension of God, a
dimension often attributed to or taken over by the Virgin Mother.
Would this be the meaning of Auden's statement, "Man is more
perfect but woman is more complete" (1958)? It is out of maternal
sheltering that the coherency speech announces comes to pass; it
is by virtue of language that the encompassing heterogeneity is
saved. In thinking one encounters the unthinkable—sometimes
an unthinkable, unsayable dimension that is, nevertheless, closer
to me than myself. It is by virtue of words, of the Word, that one
can go beyond words into a real that, at certain moments, is the
nonrational source of salvation for the speaking animal.

"Man overcomes the unthinkable of death by postulating maternal love in its place—in the place and stead of death and
thought. This love, of which divine love is merely a not always
convincing derivation, psychologically is perhaps a recall, on the
near side of early identifications, of the primal shelter that en-
sured the survival of the newborn. Such a love is in fact, logically speaking, a surge of anguish at the very moment when the
identity of thought and living body collapses. The possibilities of
communication having been swept away, only the subtle gamut
of sound, touch and visual traces, older than language and newly
worked out, are preserved as an ultimate shield against death. It
is only 'normal' for a maternal representation to set itself up at
the place of this subdued anguish called love" (pp. 176–77).

But the text then reverts to its overt emphasis on the defensiveness of the veneration of the Virgin. After a passing but thorough
rejection of anything that Freud or Jung—and possibly, by exten-

sion, any mere man—might have to say on the subject, Kristeva lists the elements (beginning with "*I* do not conceive with *you* but with *Him*," which, come to think of it, is more or less what Eve said when she had Cain ["And Adam knew Eve his wife; and she conceived and bare Cain, and said, I have gotten a man from the Lord"], at least she could be taken as saying that if one doesn't

To focus on "how" and "began" in "how it all began" is, for Beckett, in *Footfalls*, to defend against "it all . . . it all."

The age is one of evening the score, of redressing grievous wrongs. Fair enough. But redressing wrongs can cover the inevitability, beyond all rectification, of gender paranoia, gender enmity.

In the beginning? Let us not worry about what *was*, in the beginning. Better that we worry about the inevitability of enmity, quite apart from whether the chora or the phallus has the primacy of being primal; better that we worry about how enmity could be acknowledged rather than enacted; better that we worry about the chance for love in a defensively closed-over world; better if we could pray that a symbolic mother could pray for us.

It is not necessarily defen-

want to go along with the idea

that it *is* sort of miraculous)

of her case for "the virginal

maternal [as] a way . . . of

dealing with feminine para-

noia." ("Feminine paranoia" is

a much nicer, less vulgar, less

defensively phallocentering

way of phrasing what "mas-

culine paranoia" [castration

anxiety] calls penis envy. I

prefer it.)

Further elements in

Kristeva's case for the virginal

maternal as a way of dealing

sive to believe in God, and even not necessarily defensive to believe in a hereafter. Whether either is defensive or nondefensive depends on whether one's heart is in the right place. In fact, I am uncertain that symbolic participation is possible outside a conscious or unconscious literal level of participation that grounds and decenters it. The intellectual ruling-out of a literal level can be just as tyrannical as an inquisition that attempts to compel literal belief.

To tell the truth, there really isn't any way of taking things literally. The literal is a first level of figuration. First levels of figuration are interpreted by later levels, but, according to Ricoeur, the power of symbolization of subsequent levels is derived from the first.

To ground and to decenter can't be merely opposites. What is central in one perspective repeats itself as marginal and decentering in another.

Derrida pays his debts to Plato and Hegel by decentering, unfreezing them. (Though Derrida's agitation is contained in his laughter,

with feminine paranoia: "The Virgin assumes the paranoid lust for power by changing a woman into a Queen in heaven" but stifles "that megalomania by putting it on its knees before a child-god" (p. 180). "The Virgin assumes the paranoid fantasy of being excluded from time and death through the very flattering representation of Dormition or Assumption" (p. 181). The Virgin assumes "the image of A Unique Woman: alone among women, alone among mothers, alone among humans since she is without sin. But the acknowledgement of a longing

his revenge in the rigor of his reading, it is Hegel's philosophy of religion—which is to say, according to Derrida, Hegel's philosophy, the "frozen completion" of Hegel's philosophy—that agitated Kierkegaard and agitates Derrida. Hegel's attitude toward Abraham specifically was and is an affront. Without a mother and with an overinvolved, overzealous, overbiblical father, Kierkegaard grew up on and passionately in the story of Abraham and Isaac. Hegel's treatment of the father Abraham was an attack on Kierkegaard's [and, I assume, Derrida's] father and forefathers.)

for uniqueness is immediately checked . . . uniqueness is attained only through an exacerbated masochism" (p. 181).

Kristeva, positioning herself overtly with Marx, Nietzsche, and Freud, calls all of this "a skilful balance of concessions and constraints involving feminine paranoia," a "clever balanced architecture [that] today appears to be crumbling" (pp. 181, 182). However, when she moves to the question of those aspects of the feminine psyche for which the Christian representation of motherhood does not provide a solution, the picture, oddly, changes little. It

The phallus represses the chora? The phallus, the imaginary phallus, the phallus that is deployed to repress the chora, represses all that we are turning away from and all that we have turned away from. The imaginary phallus represses the abject. It is an

is as though the choices between defensive and nondefensive belief or between defensive and nondefensive disbelief can barely matter.

effort to repress undifferentiated maternality, the mother
of symbiosis, the mother as
a figure of death, the yearning for the early, life/death,
mother lost. It represses, that
is, grief, which then returns
as depression or abjection.
It is an effort to repress the
original emptiness with which
one entered the world. It is
an effort to repress desire,
or, at least, honest desire—
desire that does not deny its
origins in the original splitting, emptiness, indigence,
and guilt.

But the turning toward the
hope of wholeness and life
remains driven, empty, and
imaginary until or unless one
can, in that turning, simultaneously face the fear of lack
and death that the rejected
mother of symbiosis comes to
represent.

In ordinary development,
the mother of symbiosis, the
mother of undifferentiated
maternality, gives way to
the mother of differentiated
maternality in the place of
the Other. The symbiotic
mother gives way to the symbolic mother. By virtue of the
symbolic mother, the wish/
fear for the symbiotic mother
can be faced, renounced, and

"The unspoken doubtless

weighs first on the maternal

body: as no signifier can uplift

it without leaving a remain-

der, for the signifier is always

meaning, communication or

structure, whereas a woman

as mother would be, instead, a

strange fold that changes cul-

ture into nature, the speaking

into biology" (p. 182). And,

in the accompanying margin,

"The languages of the great

formerly matriarchal civiliza-

tions must avoid, do avoid,

personal pronouns: they leave

to the context the burden of

transcended and, thereby, one's finitude achieved.

It is through the child's turning from the symbiotic, imaginary mother to the symbolic mother that the real mother can mediate the father's assumption of the place of the Other. And only then is nondefensive phallocentrism achieved.

It is by virtue of the woman that either defensive or nondefensive phallocentrism is mediated.

Ever since Freud, psychoanalysis has been accused of seeing destiny, barring heroic efforts, as mainly set in early interactions with the mother, usually referred to, in The-Name-Of-Science (and as dim tribute to her having come into view in the aspect of what Freud called "unassimilable" thingliness) as "the object." (Nevertheless, we are saved as separate by virtue of the realness of that unassimilable thingliness from which we finally turn away. But the abject, that from which we turn away, is marked by that turning; we are marked by that turning, so that, thenceforth, a calling to and a calling from the ab-

distinguishing protagonists and take refuge in tones to recover an underwater, transverbal communication between bodies. It is a music from which so-called oriental civility tears away suddenly through violence, murder, blood baths. A woman's discourse, would that be it? Did not Christianity attempt, among other things, to freeze that see-saw? To stop it, tear women away from its rhythm, settle them permanently in the spirit? Too permanently" (pp. 182–83).

"A suffering lined with

ject is instilled. Whether that calling is heeded or stilled, whether it is heard as a calling forth or a calling back, whether it hallows or evokes horror, depends.)

In the mediation of non-defensive phallocentrism, the prior maternal gods are eclipsed by reason of womanly wisdom evolved over the millenia. That wisdom is rooted in woman's renunciation of defensively self-aggrandizing narcissism. It is a wisdom that derives from and allows for the knowledge in her bones that her offspring can become human, enter the world of language, and thereby the space of the Other, only by departing the mother/child narcissistic enclosure. So, her original role as stand-in for the Other is deployed in the service of mediating that position to the father. To reverse the direction of that mediation, which some people now advocate (without knowing *what* they advocate), could only lead to the chaos that is always the term of any enacted quest for paradise. That is why God positioned the flaming sword that turns

jubilation—ambivalence of masochism—on account of which a woman . . . allows herself a coded, fundamental, perverse behaviour . . . without which society will not reproduce and will not maintain a constancy of standardized household. . . . Feminine perversion [*père-version*] is coiled up in the desire for law as desire for reproduction and continuity, it promotes feminine masochism to the rank of structure stabilizer" (p. 183).

And, finally (in a clear allusion to Lacan's statement that "between the mother and

every which way and all those
second-order angels at the
gates of Eden.

It is not that maleness and
femaleness were originally
either each doubled within
itself or both united in one
being. (Freud didn't realize that what Aristophanes
was talking about and also
the earlier *Brihadâranyaka-
upanishad* account were
already derivative myths.
Besides, Aristophanes [Plato,
189e] was only kidding
around anyway.) Originally
there was no maleness—only
a prelinguistic, wordless, maternal procreation of only the
to-be-maternal.

Maleness (he) arose as a
differentiation within the
maternal, and only then, with
the differentiation and establishment of man *and* woman,
did God, the God of word
and world, appear. (Maternality, as such, is wordless
and worldless.)

Before God created the
worldhood of the world, before He created man and
woman, before God "ap-
peared," before there was
any "one" to whom God
could appear, maternality was

the child, Freud introduced

a third term . . . the phal-

lus," and to the function of

the father in changing the

relationship between mother,

child, phallus), "repudiation

of the other sex (the mascu-

line) no longer seems possible

under the aegis of the third

person, hypostatized in the

child as go-between: 'neither

me, nor you, but him, the

child, the third person, the

non-person, God, which I still

am in the final analysis. . . .'

Since there is repudiation,

and if the feminine being that

struggles within it is to remain

always already there. The
meaning of God's maleness is
that God, language, the worldhood of the world, and man
appeared together. One might
call it guilt by association.

By virtue of the differentiation of maleness, woman
appeared, as woman, out of
the maternal. Man derived
from the maternal but so did
woman. Woman owes her
being as woman to man's
appearance.

Adam was created first.
That his rib was located in
Eve is mythical tribute to
maternality as source and
to woman's less clear-cut
differentiation from undifferentiated maternality.

Adam was created first
and was the first to speak, to
name, but woman was the first
to know.

Woman, closer to the ma-
ternal, always already knows.
For her, eating, knowing in
whatever way, and feeding
are, virtually, natural.

Woman, closer to the ma-
ternal, is used to being. Man,
newly created, is more concerned about his being, has
a deeper sense of being cut
off, is more anxious, prone
to guilt, less given to griev-

there, it henceforth calls for,

not the deification of the third

party, but counter-cathexes

in strong values, in strong

equivalents of power. Feminine

psychosis today is sustained

and absorbed through passion

for politics, science, art. . . .

The variant that accompanies

motherhood might be ana-

lysed perhaps more readily

than the others from the stand-

point of the rejection of the

other sex that it compromises.

To allow what? Surely not

some understanding or other

on the part of 'sexual partners'

within the pre-established haring, and puzzled and aghast at what the woman knows. (Would Eve have freely offered the apple if *she* were overcome with shame and guilt? *They* became ashamed after *he* ate.)

The education of woman by man is toward awakening in her the guilt, shame, and fear of the maternal that *he* thinks she *ought* to feel. If God had walked into that scene as a Mother, Adam would have surely died. For Adam's sake (but also for Eve's), God *had* to be a Father.

Man, by reason of being more cut off, is both more driven toward reunion with the maternal and more frightened of it.

Even so, both man and woman are cut off. Both seek and fear reunion. Through the yearning and enmity set, in cleaving to, uniting with, each other, femaleness and maleness are brought together again in reserved, ritual tribute to maternality as source and destiny, life and death.

It was Eve, coming to be as still within the to-be-maternal, who first opened her eyes to the knowledge of good and evil. It's just that

mony of primary androgyny" (p. 184).

Is this the bitter fruit of demythologization? There is nothing in it that could be seen as reason for feminine exultation in liberation. Man is given Hell, but woman and man remain in misery. It is a grim recapitulation of expulsion from Eden, but this time with man more to blame than the woman and with no serpent as final alibi.

Maybe, in large part, that is just the way it is. But can this overt statement be taken as Kristeva's position? I doubt it.

she, in need of education, was less overwhelmed by it all.

The serpent is maleness still within maternality. The "subtil" serpent—only the spelling of the King James version will do: the subtil is capable of making or noticing fine distinctions in meaning (a subtil thinker); marked by or requiring mental keenness; delicately skillful or clever; deft or ingenious; not open or direct; crafty; sly; delicately suggestive, not grossly obvious; working insidiously; not easily detected (a subtil poison)—the subtil serpent is undifferentiated maternality.

The serpent is the only one of this particular trinity who is not asked about what transpired. Undifferentiated maternality (nature) needs no alibi. God asked Adam, then He asked Eve, then He cursed all three.

The enmity set between the serpent and woman sealed, at once, the differentiation of maleness and maternality, of man and woman, but especially the differentiation of femaleness and maternality— of the woman and her mother. It barred the reabsorption of woman within the maternal. Henceforth, in this division,

Over against this position, there is a concept of the symbolic mother at work in the deep structure of both the text and margins of Kristeva's "Stabat Mater," even though the symbolic mother is a concept from which Kristeva is superficially barred by reason of her emphasis on the semiotic versus the "allmightiness" (p. 185) of the symbolic, the chora versus language, and of an "herethics" versus defensively exploitative phallocentrism. The war, to be sure, is there: the enmity is set. The enmity and the warfare neither the labor of man nor the labor of woman would be easy, or even natural.

To be in the world is to be differentiated (from the serpent, from maternality— for the woman, from maleness as the serpent within). The differentiation of a subject is inaugurated by and forever anchored in the differentiation of gender. What is feared and wished for by man, feared because wished for, is not woman but undifferentiated maternality—reentry into undifferentiated maternality. Woman, to man, can represent undifferentiated maternality. But woman as mother, by also representing the Other, offers a way out—to the male gods, to a male God.

Kristeva is, all mothers are, sad that this should be their child's destiny. But she/they know it is the only way their daughters can become women and their sons men; it is the only way there can be a return to the mother as woman, to the mother as differentiated maternality, or to the mother as symbolic mother, or to woman as woman.

are overtly acknowledged in Kristeva's main text.

The approach to a foreign religion (or to a religion that one has renounced) tends to be an approach in which one first sees the possibilities of defense. Kristeva and most psychoanalysts, would, in this respect, be following Freud (and Marx and Nietzsche). However, it is my assertion that traversing the oedipal period—the assumption of gender, the assumption of subjecthood, and entry into

Gender is the sexually differentiated animal's celebration of being as animal in a world opened by the Other, a phallocentric world, always undermined and renewed, questioned and upheld, deconstructed and sustained by maternality as source, by the maternal presence within the Other.

The coming of the child challenges, changes, triangulates, and sometimes secures the marital recapitulation of dyadic love. The child, boy or girl, is, in this sense, the father, the third party in the place of the Other, a miraculous incarnation of the divine, that intervenes in the marital dyad.

Achieving a new level of love or being is to repeat, to go back to original love and being in the right way. Maternal love for a son is everything Freud thought and Kristeva thinks, not just because opposites attract, or because the son is her phallus, or the baby of her father, or the solution of feminine paranoia, or the third party that triangulates and secures the marital dyad. The son is the maleness from which

the symbolic order—allows for nondefensive access to both a symbolic father and a symbolic mother.

It is not feminine masochism alone that is a "structure stabilizer." It is neither the chora alone nor the symbolic function alone, neither the maternal function nor metaphor alone, nor the paternal function or metaphor alone, that stabilizes human existence. Ultimately, it is the autonomy doubly guaranteed by the drives and one's apparatuses for attunement to external reality that stabilizes.

the mother has differentiated in order to *be* a woman. The woman celebrates her womanhood through the son. The son born of her womb is, more than the daughter, the loss of her own undifferentiated maternality accomplished in primary maternal preoccupation; he becomes the object of her (renounced) yearning for her early, undifferentiated male/female, symbiotic mother. The fullness of her renounced love for that mother can be given to her son.

This is the burden, the cross, the double cross—to be loved as a son is to be loved as the mother's mother—that sons, more than daughters, bear. If the son can die to all that, he achieves not divinity but his humanity. If he can't, he is fated to remain divine. And just as the critical factor in a psychoanalytic cure is the resolution of the countertransference neurosis, the critical factor in the son's dying to/separating from the mother is the mother's renunciation of primary narcissistic love regained (repeated) in pregnancy and childbirth.

It is a curious dying. It is a dying to narcissistic love, to

But this stability is realized and brought to fruition for an "I" by virtue of entry into the symbolic order that has been mediated first by the symbolic mother and then by the symbolic father. Entry into the symbolic order (the law, language, the space of the Other) then allows nondefensive access at a higher level to the symbolic mother or father.

What Kristeva knows in her margins is that the mother's adoration of the child anticipates and opens the way for the child's adoration of the mother. The mother nondefensively participates in the primary

the divine, to the original way of participating in the eternal that allows for nondefensive return to that way of being in certain modes of regression and identification, in love, in illness, and in the face of death.

identificatory love by virtue of being specially equipped with the capacity for primary maternal preoccupation. Her adoration mediates the reciprocal adoration through which the child has access to the symbolic mother—the mother as representative of the Other. What Kristeva knows marginally is that not every quest for the symbolic mother is a defensive return to archaic symbiosis nor, for the girl, a solution to feminine paranoia. Not every regression is narrowly defensive. There is also regression in the service of being more fully within the space of the Other.

It is not a defect of the symbol that it symbolizes not only the Other (every symbol, no matter what it represents, is also a symbol of symbolization) but also the real. A symbol—the symbolic order—is the way in which the real becomes known as real; the real mother as "unassimilable . . . thing" (Freud, *Standard Edition*, 1:366) is mediated by the mother in the place of the Other. The literal level of the mother as symbol is anchored in the real mother, known *as* real.

It is no defect of the symbolic mother, of Mary as symbol, of Mary as symbolic mother, that she symbolizes not only the Other,

The infant knows right off its mother, by smell, taste, sight, touch, and sound. But it doesn't know that it knows her. Apparatuses of primary autonomy grant awareness, but not awareness of awareness.

This look smell tone way

but also, even if by way of negation or disavowal, the flesh-and-blood real mother.

In the case of Mary, the deletion of flesh and blood, of sex and death, can represent of holding mood blurred percept of lips nipple hair song humming warmth of milk urine feces is gradually punctuated into a perceptually effective her/me within oneness.

At eight months she appears, whole, and along with her, the stranger, and anxiety. And then the whole issue of identity of perception or identity of thought, effectively traversed (but within awareness to the first power only) approximately seven and one-half months earlier, is thrown into question by a primitive, prelinguistic awareness of awareness and has to be reworked.

Her? or her image? Her actual touch or a wanting that remembers? and does it matter? Either one beats the dread of the stranger or of wanting alone. It matters.

What stabilizes the question of her or her image that arises anew within awareness to the second power is the appearance there of "me." The question of me or my image doesn't yet arise. My image, mirrored, of course, by her, but that will do.

"I" arrive in awe. It is in primitive wonder and awe

and, no doubt, in some measure always does represent, a defense against incest and death, and for the woman, a solution of "feminine paranoia." However, such would not exhaust the meaning of Mary as symbol. It would not foreclose the possibility of a nondefensive return to the archaic symbolic mother or to Mary as symbol of the archaic symbolic mother. This return could be an experience of the eternal that would remove the sting of death, sustain one in the face of the emptiness that the word, and love, and "I" can appear. The beginning is marked by awe, the word, and love, each of which generates the others—each of which (almost) is the others. It is thus that "I" arrive on the scene of awareness of awareness. "I" have a position from which "I" can (almost) speak. "I" am, "she" is, "we" are, as one. "My" hand, "my" head, "my" body, moving at "my" will, just like hers. It's a start. patch

To paraphrase: The rock irregular lichened mud-red to ash grey cinder sharp above the vegetation is slow to crumble. Only at the base here and there through time has it given way to sand. But between the crest and shore, in the bright sun, myriads of flowers shine.

of death.

The deletion of sex and

death could represent, symbolically, a nondefensive acknowledgment of the mother

as separate and apart from

the "I" and its most central

desires and fears. The deletion

of sex and death could also be

a nondefensive acknowledgment of the interimplications

of sex and death. It could also

be a nondefensive mode of emphasizing the importance of the mother as original stand-in for the Other; it could be a way of seeing that it is as the symbolic mother that she gives the life or death that counts.

REFERENCES

Auden, W. H. 1958. "A history-making animal." Washington School of Psychiatry lecture.

Beckett, Samuel. 1981. *Footfalls.* In *Ends and Odds: Nine Dramatic Pieces by Samuel Beckett.* New York: Grove, pp. 39–49.

Bloom, Harold. 1973. *The Anxiety of Influence.* London: Oxford University Press.

———. 1980. Freud's concept of defense and the poetic will. In *The Literary Freud: Mechanisms of Defense and the Poetic Will,* vol. 4 of *Psychiatry and the Humanities,* ed. Joseph Smith. New Haven: Yale University Press, pp. 1–28.

Chomsky, Noam. 1968. *Language and Mind.* New York: Harcourt Brace Jovanovich.

———. 1978. Language and unconscious knowledge. In *Psychoanalysis and Language,* vol. 3 of *Psychiatry and the Humanities,* ed. Joseph Smith. New Haven: Yale University Press, pp. 3–44.

Derrida, Jacques. 1987. *The Post Card: From Socrates to Freud and Beyond.* Trans. with an introduction and notes by Alan Bass. Chicago: University of Chicago Press.

Edelson, Marshall. 1975. *Language and Interpretation in Psychoanalysis.* New Haven: Yale University Press.

Eliot, T. S. 1950. Tradition and the individual talent. In *Selected Essays by T. S. Eliot.* New York: Harcourt Brace Jovanovich, pp. 3–11.

Felman, Shoshana. 1987. *Jacques Lacan and the Adventure of Insight: Psychoanalysis in Contemporary Culture.* Cambridge: Harvard University Press.

Fox, Richard. 1984. The principle of abstinence reconsidered. *International Review of Psycho-Analysis* 11:227–36.

Freud, Sigmund. 1953–64. *Standard Edition of the Complete Psychological Works,* 24 vols., ed. James Strachey. London: Hogarth Press.

———. 1895. Project for a scientific psychology. *Standard Edition*, 1:283–397.

———. 1900a. *The Interpretation of Dreams*. Trans. A. A. Brill. In *The Basic Writings of Sigmund Freud*. New York: Modern Library, 1938, 179–549.

———. 1900b. *The Interpretation of Dreams*. Standard Edition, 4 and 5.

———. 1901. *The Psychopathology of Everyday Life*. Standard Edition, 6.

———. 1905. *Jokes and Their Relation to the Unconscious*. Standard Edition, 8:9–236.

———. 1907. Delusions and dreams in Jensen's *Gradiva*. Standard Edition, 9:7–95.

———. 1909. Notes upon a case of obsessional neurosis. Standard Edition, 10:153–318.

———. 1911. Formulation on the two principles of mental functioning. *Standard Edition*, 12:218–26.

———. 1912. On the universal tendency to debasement in the sphere of love. *Standard Edition*, 11:179–90.

———. 1913. *Totem and Taboo*. Standard Edition, 13:1–162.

———. 1914. On narcissism: An introduction. *Standard Edition*, 14:73–102.

———. 1915a. Instincts and their vicissitudes. *Standard Edition*, 14:117–40.

———. 1915b. Repression. *Standard Edition*, 14:145–58.

———. 1915c. The unconscious. *Standard Edition*, 14:166–215.

———. 1915d. The unconscious. *Collected Papers*, 4:98–136.

———. 1921. *Group Psychology and the Analysis of the Ego. Standard Edition*, 18:69–143.

———. 1923. *The Ego and the Id. Standard Edition*, 19:12–66.

———. 1925. Negation. *Standard Edition*, 19:234–39.

———. 1926. *Inhibitions, Symptoms, and Anxiety. Standard Edition*, 20:87–172.

———. 1930. *Civilization and Its Discontents. Standard Edition*, 21:64–145.

———. 1933. *New Introductory Lectures on Psycho-Analysis. Standard Edition*, 22:5–157.

———. 1940a. *An Outline of Psycho-Analysis. Standard Edition*, 23:144–207.

———. 1940b. Some elementary lessons in psycho-analysis. *Standard Edition*, 23:279–86.

Gallop, Jane. 1981. Phallus/penis: Same difference. In *Men by Women*, vol. 2 of *Women and Literature* (new series), ed. Janet Todd. New York: Holmes and Meier, pp. 243–51.

—————. 1985. *Reading Lacan.* Ithaca: Cornell University Press.

Gill, Merton. 1963. *Topography and Systems in Psychoanalytic Theory,* vol. 3 of *Psychological Issues.*

Green, André. 1983. The logic of Lacan's *objet a* and Freudian theory: Convergences and questions. Trans. Kimberly Kleinert [Lungociu] and Beryl Schlossman. In *Interpreting Lacan,* vol. 6 of *Psychiatry and the Humanities,* ed. Joseph Smith and William Kerrigan. New Haven: Yale University Press, pp. 161–91.

Hartmann, Heinz. 1956. Notes on the reality principle. In *Essays on Ego Psychology.* New York: International Universities Press, pp. 241–67.

Heidegger, Martin. 1962. *Being and Time.* Trans. John Macquarrie and Edward Robinson. New York: Harper & Row.

Kerrigan, William. 1983. Introduction to *Interpreting Lacan,* vol. 6 of *Psychiatry and the Humanities,* ed. Joseph Smith and William Kerrigan. New Haven: Yale University Press, pp. ix–xxvii.

Kierkegaard, Søren. 1941. *Repetition: An Essay in Experimental Psychology.* Trans. with an introduction and notes by Walter Lowrie. New York: Harper Torchbooks.

—————. 1954. *Fear and Trembling.* Trans. with introductions and notes by Walter Lowrie. New York: Doubleday Anchor Books.

Klein, George. 1967. Peremptory ideation: Structure and force in motivated ideas. *Psychological Issues* 5:80–128.

Kohut, Heinz. 1971. *The Analysis of the Self.* New York: International Universities Press.

—————. 1979. The two analyses of Mr. Z. *International Journal of Psycho-Analysis* 60:3–27.

Kris, Ernst. 1950. On preconscious mental processes. *Psychoanalytic Quarterly* 19:540–60.

Kristeva, Julia. 1982. *Powers of Horror.* Trans. Leon Roudiez. New York: Columbia University Press.

—————. 1983. Within the microcosm of "the talking cure." Trans. Thomas Gora and Margaret Waller. In *Interpreting Lacan,* vol. 6 of *Psychiatry and the Humanities,* ed. Joseph Smith and William Kerrigan. New Haven: Yale University Press, pp. 33–48.

—————. 1986. *The Kristeva Reader.* Ed. Toril Moi. New York: Columbia University Press.

—————. 1987a. *In the Beginning Was Love: Psychoanalysis and Faith.* Trans.

Arthur Goldhammer, with an introduction by Otto F. Kernberg. New York: Columbia University Press.

———. 1987b. *Tales of Love*. Trans. Leon Roudiez. New York: Columbia University Press.

Lacan, Jacques. 1968. *The Language of the Self*. Trans. Anthony Wilden. Baltimore: Johns Hopkins University Press.

———. 1975. *Encore, Séminaire XX* (1972–73). Ed. Jacques-Alain Miller. Paris: Edition du Seuil.

———. 1977a. *Ecrits*. Trans. Alan Sheridan. New York: W.W. Norton.

———. 1977b. *Ornicar?* 10:5–12 (session for 13 April 1976).

———. 1978a. *The Four Fundamental Concepts of Psycho-Analysis*. Trans. Alan Sheridan and ed. Jacques-Alain Miller. New York: W.W. Norton.

———. 1978b. *Lacan in Italia, 1973–1978*. Ed. Giacomo Contri. Milan: La Salamandra.

———. 1988a. *The Seminar of Jacques Lacan*, vol. 1, *Freud's Papers on Technique, 1953–1954*, ed. Jacques-Alain Miller. Trans. with notes by John Forrester. New York: W.W. Norton.

———. 1988b. *The Seminar of Jacques Lacan*, vol. 2, *The Ego in Freud's Theory and in the Technique of Psychoanalysis, 1954–1955*, ed. Jacques-Alain Miller. Trans. Sylvana Tomaselli with notes by John Forrester. New York: W.W. Norton.

Laplanche, Jean. 1976. *Life and Death in Psychoanalysis*. Trans. Jeffrey Mehlman. Baltimore: Johns Hopkins University Press.

Laplanche, Jean, and J.-B. Pontalis. 1973. *The Language of Psycho-Analysis*. Trans. Donald Nicholas-Smith. New York: W.W. Norton.

Loewald, Hans. 1973. Review of *The Analysis of the Self*. *Psychoanalytic Quarterly* 42:441–51.

———. 1978. *Psychoanalysis and the History of the Individual*. New Haven: Yale University Press.

———. 1980. On the therapeutic action of psychoanalysis. In *Papers on Psychoanalysis*. New Haven: Yale University Press, pp. 221–56.

Muller, John. 1989. Lacan and Kohut: From imaginary to symbolic identification in the case of Mr. Z. In *Self Psychology: Comparison and Contrast*, ed. Douglas Detrick and Susan Detrick. Hillsdale, N.J.: Analytic Press, pp. 363–94.

Muller, John, and William Richardson. 1982. *Lacan and Language: A Reader's Guide to* Ecrits. New York: International Universities Press.

Piaget, Jean. 1971a. *Insights and Illusions of Philosophy*. Trans. Wolfe Mays. New York: World Publishing Company.

———. 1971b. *Structuralism*. Trans. and ed. Chaninah Maschler. New York: Harper Torchbooks.

———. 1973. The affective unconscious and the cognitive unconscious. *Journal of the American Psychoanalytic Association* 21:249–61.

Rapaport, David. 1953. On the psychoanalytic theory of affects. In *The Collected Papers of David Rapaport*, ed. Merton Gill. New York: Basic Books, 1967, pp. 476–512.

———. 1957. The theory of ego autonomy. In *The Collected Papers of David Rapaport*, ed. Merton Gill. New York: Basic Books, 1967, pp. 722–44.

———. 1957–59. *Seminars on Elementary Metapsychology*. 3 vols. Transcripts of seminars held at Austen Riggs Center.

———. 1960. On the psychoanalytic theory of motivation. In *The Collected Papers of David Rapaport*, ed. Merton Gill. New York: Basic Books, 1967, pp. 853–915.

Rapaport, David, and Merton Gill. 1959. The points of view and assumptions of metapsychology. In *The Collected Papers of David Rapaport*, ed. Merton Gill. New York: Basic Books, 1967, pp. 795–811.

Ricoeur, Paul. 1970. *Freud and Philosophy: An Essay in Interpretation*. Trans. Denis Savage. New Haven: Yale University Press.

———. 1978. Image and language in psychoanalysis. In *Psychoanalysis and Language*, vol. 3 of *Psychiatry and the Humanities*, ed. Joseph Smith. New Haven: Yale University Press, pp. 293–324.

Rorty, Richard. 1986. Freud and moral reflection. In *Pragmatism's Freud: The Moral Disposition of Psychoanalysis*, vol. 9 of *Psychiatry and the Humanities*, ed. Joseph Smith and William Kerrigan. Baltimore: Johns Hopkins University Press, pp. 1–27.

Schafer, Roy. 1968. *Aspects of Internalization*. New York: International Universities Press.

Schur, Max. 1953. The ego in anxiety. In *Drives, Affects, Behaviour*, vol. 1, ed. Rudolph Loewenstein. New York: International Universities Press, pp. 67–103.

Smith, Joseph. 1970. On the structural view of affect. *Journal of the American Psychoanalytic Association* 18:539–61.

———. 1971. Identificatory styles in depression and grief. *International Journal of Psycho-Analysis* 52:259–66.

———. 1976. Language and the genealogy of the absent object. In *Psychiatry and the Humanities*, vol. 1, ed. Joseph Smith. New Haven: Yale University Press, pp. 145–70.

————. 1977. The pleasure principle. *International Journal of Psycho-Analysis* 58:1–10.

————. 1978. Introduction to *Psychoanalysis and Language*, vol. 3 of *Psychiatry and the Humanities*, ed. Joseph Smith. New Haven: Yale University Press, pp. ix–xxx.

————. 1980a. Fathers and daughters. *Man and World* 13:385–402.

————. 1980b. Introduction to *The Literary Freud: Mechanisms of Defense and the Poetic Will*, vol. 4 of *Psychiatry and the Humanities*, ed. Joseph Smith. New Haven: Yale University Press, pp. ix–xix.

————. 1983. Rite, ritual, and defense. *Psychiatry* 46:16–30.

————. 1986a. Dualism revisited: Schafer, Hartmann, and Freud. *Psychoanalytic Inquiry* 6:543–73.

————. 1986b. Primitive guilt. In *Pragmatism's Freud: The Moral Disposition of Psychoanalysis*, vol. 9 of *Psychiatry and the Humanities*, ed. Joseph Smith and William Kerrigan. Baltimore: Johns Hopkins University Press, pp. 52–78.

————. 1989. Evening the score. *Modern Language Notes* 104:1050–65.

————. 1991. Ego psychology and the language of Lacan: Transference and affect. *Psychoanalysis and Contemporary Thought* 14, no. 1.

Smith, Joseph, Ping-Nie Pao, and Noel Schweig. 1973. On the concept of aggression. *Psychoanalytic Study of the Child* 28:331–46.

Stern, Daniel. 1985. *The Interpersonal World of the Infant: A View from Psychoanalysis and Developmental Psychology*. New York: Basic Books.

Vergote, Antoine. 1983. From Freud's "Other Scene" to Lacan's "Other." Trans. Thomas Acklin and Beryl Schlossman. In *Interpreting Lacan*, vol. 6 of *Psychiatry and the Humanities*, ed. Joseph Smith and William Kerrigan. New Haven: Yale University Press, pp. 193–221.

Viorst, Judith. 1986. *Necessary Losses*. New York: Simon and Schuster.

Waelder, Robert. 1936. The principle of multiple function: Observations on over-determination. *Psychoanalytic Quarterly* 5:5–62.

INDEX

Abject, 112, 121, 125, 127
Abstinence, 68
Adam, 130
Advanced and primitive modes in primary process, 9, 97
Affect, 23, 32, 45; as conscious ego response, 88; as *de novo* response, 85; pleasure principle and, 81, 87–89; as representative of drive, 86–87; repression and, 83–84; signification and, 13, 79–80, 83–85, 87; structural view of, 85; unconscious, 83–84
Affective recognition, 85–89
Affective unpleasure, 81
Agency, pleasure principle and, 34
Aggression, 53, 82
American ego psychology, 4–9, 53–54, 57–58; Lacan's view of, 4–9, 53–54, 62–63, 87
Anxiety, 12, 83, 85, 88, 97, 137; castration, 77; defense and, 52–53; as response to danger, 51–52; sexual drive and, 51–52
Aristophanes, 129
Art, abject as source of, 121
Auden, W. H., 122

Autoerotic phase, 21
Autonomy, 34, 45, 47, 82, 134

Beauvoir, Simone de, 113
Beckett, Samuel, 123
Behavior, directionality of, 3
Being, want of, 70–71
Binarism, pleasure principle and, 81–82
Bloom, Harold, 16–17, 64, 97

Castration. *See* Symbolic castration
Castration anxiety, 77
Chomsky, Noam, 1, 3, 16, 19, 20, 49
Chora, the, 111–12, 117–21, 123, 125, 132, 134
Cognitive unconscious, 19
Consciousness, 33, 68, 73, 84; language and, 19; psychical and, 19–20; unconscious knowledge and, 29–31
Countertransference, 66, 135
Cure, 89–94

Danger, 11, 29, 47, 56, 63, 69, 81, 83, 84, 92, 97–98, 105, 116; anxiety as response to, 51–52;

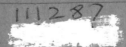